THE MYSTERY OF SUFFERING

THE MYSTER OF SUFFERING

TO
MARGARET

The Mystery of Suffering

by

HUGH EVAN HOPKINS

INTER-VARSITY PRESS
1519 NORTH ASTOR, CHICAGO 10,
ILLINOIS

© The Inter-Varsity Fellowship

First Edition . . *June* 1959

PRINTED AND BOUND IN ENGLAND BY
HAZELL WATSON AND VINEY LTD
AYLESBURY AND SLOUGH

CONTENTS

Scripture quotations from the Revised .... version of the bible [copyrighted] 19[58] and 19[52] by the Division of Christian Education, National Council of Churches, U.S.A. are used by permission.

ACKNOWLEDGEMENT

Scripture quotations from the Revised Standard Version of the Bible (copyrighted 1946 and 1952 by the Division of Christian Education, National Council of Churches, U.S.A.) are used by permission.

FOREWORD

I HAVE TRIED in this small book to look at the mystery of suffering in the light of the Bible. Having done this, the whole subject remains a mystery to me, but I have received such help and inspiration from studying what the Scriptures say about it that I feel I must try to share some of these good things with others. This is by no means a theological treatise. It is simply a modest attempt to look at the chief passages in the Bible which deal with this topic of suffering and pain by one whose great joy has been trying to help those who are up against things to face life with their faith strengthened and their devotion to our Lord deepened.

I have quoted throughout from the latest translation of the Bible, the Revised Standard Version, which is generally accepted as the most accurate and intelligible of our day. It would help if a copy of the Bible was near at hand for reference, but the passages have mostly been printed in full.

It will be obvious how deeply indebted I am to the many writers on this subject from whose books fresh light has come to me from time to time. Even more deep is my debt to those men and women whom I have met in the course of my ministry in India, East Africa and Britain, whose example and fellowship have shown me something of the true Christian attitude to suffering.

H.A.E.H.

Cheltenham, 1959.

PROLOGUE

PROLOGUE

THE butterfly, which in Kipling's poem preached contentment from the roadside to the unfortunate toad as it trembled under the threat of the farmer's harrow, is a warning to all who consider seriously the problems which pain and suffering present to thoughtful people. To those actually in trouble, for instance, the subject is too pressing to be a problem, and they naturally resent, as Job did, serene advice coming to them from any whose lives have never yet been scarred. For them affliction is something to be endured, not argued about; a pain to bear, not a conundrum to answer. When one's head is bowed in travail, no preacher, no minister, no friend is going to be welcome who comes with a clear-cut 'answer' to the whys and wherefores of the sufferer's troubles. That is not the time for reading about or listening to views on pain. The sufferer will want to be quiet with God then.

On the other hand, the 'butterflies' of life who are not bothered with a serious belief in God and who flit from one patch of enjoyable living to the next, who sometimes seem favoured by Providence with more than their fair share of comfort and ease—they do not find pain a problem either. Like Tennyson's gods, much envied by the Lotus-eaters, 'careless of mankind' they recline on the Elysian hills of their untroubled existence and thoughtlessly

smile in secret, looking over wasted lands,
Blight and famine, plague and earthquake, roaring deeps and fiery sands,
Clanging fights, and flaming towns, and sinking ships, and praying hands.

One day trouble will undoubtedly break up the illusion of their well-being, and they will then search around in desperation for a faith that can explain or a strength that can help them to endure. But, at present, while their lives remain undisturbed, they will not be reading this or any book that tries to reach to the deeper places of life. 'They jest at scars who never felt a wound.'

There are also those who like to exercise their intellectual abilities by sorties into the realms of the unknown. To them, the apparent irreconcilability of the existence at the same time of a good God and a suffering humanity can provide endless scope for academic acrobatics. Groups of thoughtful, though perhaps not particularly reverent, young people will let the shadows lengthen hour after hour as they discuss together 'the problem of suffering'. But evermore they come out by the same door as they entered, little better for the exercise.

> Oft in the pleasant summer years,
> Reading the tales of days bygone
> I have mused on the story of human tears,
> All that man unto man has done:
> Massacre, torture and black despair;
> Reading it all in my easy chair.

But the aches of a tortured world are not fit matter for leisurely reading or discussion. Of course, it may be that if we clothed every tragedy which the daily Press presents to us on our breakfast table with too vivid an imagination, the resultant burden would drive us to distraction. But on the other hand, we must beware lest familiarity with the existence of suffering in our present age makes us insensitive and merely curious. We should then be hardly fitted to help a friend in need, and quite unprepared to face the real challenge to Christian faith which undoubtedly does arise from the presence of pain in God's world. It is notable that Jesus Christ Himself seems to have deliberately avoided becoming entangled in argument and, when faced by challenges to rational belief in God, seldom answered questions. His way was rather to deal with what lay behind the question. He sought the motive of the questioner, and tried to deal with the matter there. We would be wise to follow His example as much as we are able.

Yet calamity certainly presents a challenge which cannot be avoided. There are numbers of our fellow-men who stand hindered on their path to God by the over-shadowing cloud of mystery which surrounds this subject. We Christians cannot but be deeply concerned at this. We are bound, as evangelists, to do all we can, either to dispel some of the mystery, or at least to show our fellow-feeling with those whose honest doubt has brought them to a halt. Any of us may at any time come across someone whose faith is fresh, but not perhaps deeply rooted, and, after the pattern of our Lord's parable, is beginning to wither away under the cruel glare of personal trouble; 'As for what was sown on rocky ground, this is he who hears the word and immediately receives it with joy; yet he has no root in himself, but endures for a while, and when tribulation or persecution arises on account of the word, immediately he falls away' (Mt. xiii. 20, 21). We cannot as Christians stand by and see our fellows drifting away from faith in God like that. In so far as we have a faith that enables us to go on believing, even in face of the apparently inexplicable, so far shall we try to share this with our enquiring friend or our troubled Christian believer. Without expecting to receive or daring to offer any facile solution to a problem that has baffled thinkers of all ages, we yet feel that, as Christians in a suffering world, we are not intended to remain as mystified as those who have no faith, or who do not care. Therefore, what light we can discover in the Bible we shall use to guide our own thinking and, we hope, to encourage others. We have a duty in the fellowship of Christ's Church to stand by and strengthen our brethren against the day of their suffering. 'Remember those who are in prison, as though in prison with them; and those who are ill-treated, since you also are in the body' (Heb. xiii. 3). Oswald Chambers, in his searching book *Baffled to Fight Better*—a book of addresses given during the war to troops in the hell of personal insecurity and fear—expounds that book of the Bible which concentrates upon the problems of suffering. He points out how the distress of Job, a man of exemplary faith and great endurance, was aggravated intensely by his personal loneliness. His wife, upon whom he might well have counted to give him comradeship and real understanding, failed to be a companion in tribulation. In addition, his friends had deserted him, and those who called themselves his 'comforters' produced intellectual panaceas which proved them to be, as Job said, 'physicians of no value'. What he needed, and what every real sufferer needs, is not someone to tell him to cheer up because things might be worse but, in the words of Oswald Cham-

bers, someone who will stand beside him and say, 'I don't
see why you are going through this; it is black and
desperate, but I will wait with you.' When our Lord Himself looked for such companionship, His closest friends,
mystified beyond description, failed to keep watch, and
left their Master to suffer alone in the darkness of the
garden, alone in the mockery of His trial, alone in the
pains of the cross. One thing you and I may be sure of is
that when we suffer, however much our friends may fail,
He will never leave us to suffer alone, nor will He fail to
help us in our need. In the strongest negative to be found
in the Greek of the New Testament, we read, 'He has said,
I will never let go of you nor will I ever in any way leave
you in the lurch' (Heb. xiii. 5, Gk.). In that confidence we
will see if we can learn enough about this great subject to
ensure that, in the day of our trial, we shall not ourselves
be found among the faithless.

CHAPTER I

GOD IS GOOD

IN his famous Essay on Nature, John Stuart Mill clearly set out the problem with which thinkers all through history have wrestled. 'If the law of all creation were justice and the Creator omnipotent, then in whatever amount suffering and happiness might be dispensed to the world, each person's share of them would be exactly proportioned to that person's good or evil deeds; no human being would have a worse lot than another, without worse deserts; accident or favouritism would have no part in such a world, but every human life would be the playing out of a drama constructed like a perfect moral tale. . . . Not even on the most distorted and contracted theory of good which ever was framed by religious or philosophical fanaticism, can the government of Nature be made to resemble the work of a being at once good or omnipotent.' [1]

The problem arises largely from the belief that a 'good' God would reward each man according to his deserts, and an 'almighty' God would have no difficulty in carrying this out. The fact that rewards and punishments in the way of happiness and discomfort appear to be haphazardly distributed in this life drives many to question either the goodness of God or His power.

If we examine the content of the words 'good' and 'omnipotent', the problem becomes less difficult than some people make it out to be. What do we mean when we declare our faith that God is 'good'? Would it in fact be a sign of God's goodness if He were to reward every man according to his behaviour? Quite apart from any happiness that might follow our goodness, where would any of us be if we received in this life an exact recompense in terms of suffering for every sin we have committed? It may well be that justice seen through human eyes might organize things in that way. But the goodness of God consists not only of justice, but also, to our infinite relief, of mercy. We know that by the loving-kindness of God, to

[1] J. S. Mill, *Essays*, p. 38.

use that very suggestive Old Testament word, whatever we do suffer, it is far less than we deserve. Indeed, the gospel message is that God's love spares us the awful prospect of receiving the due reward of our misdeeds.

P. T. Forsyth has done a great service in his book *The Justification of God* by pointing out at the start that there is really no reason at all why the God of all creation should justify Himself before men, nor is it right and proper for us His creatures to bring God's actions to the bar of our reason and expect Him to explain Himself to us. That would be gross impertinence on our part. What that great theologian does is to show how 'God vindicates His justice by saving man from the doubt of it, and not by demonstrating to him the truth of it'.[1] In the course of doing this he points out how the existence of apparent injustice in the world presents a problem to us only because we have wrong ideas about God. We think of Him today as 'a tender God in no sense judge, more kindly than holy'. This may be because we are a softer generation, and have patterned our God to our own inclinations. Our religion, like that of Bunyan's Mr. By-Ends, walks about too much, perhaps, 'in golden slippers, in the sunshine, and with applause'. God, we imagine, is easy-going and only wants His children to enjoy themselves. But this is thinking of Him in too weak terms. The idea that a loving father always wishes his children to be comfortable is refuted after all even by the humblest human standards. C. S. Lewis points out, in his book *The Problem of Pain*, that it is our faulty ideas of what God's goodness and love demand that lead us to think of happiness in terms of comfort, and human suffering as a sure sign of God's incompetence. It is essential to grasp at the outset that true happiness, as distinguished from mere enjoyment, is not irreconcilable with suffering. The perpetual enjoyment of humanity is nowhere, in the realm of revealed religion, declared to be the supreme good. If it were so, then the argument that somehow God, in allowing us to be frequently unhappy, is defeated in His aims, might be a strong one. There is, however, nothing particularly good about enjoyment. It is pleasant, but not moral. It is the result of pleasing circumstances, not necessarily the

[1] Introduction, p. vi.

sign of divine blessing. There is something far more important, and that is the formation of character and one's personal relationship with God. Because of this we can expect a good, just and loving God so to overrule the affairs of His children that, given their co-operation, this vital part of their lives can be developed, even though it may involve some curb on their pleasure.

The 'goodness' of God, then, does not consist in a desire to cushion His children from the hardships and pains of life, but in a providential interest in us, which we can trace in the Bible and experience in our personal lives, aimed at our moral development. All the same, it must be admitted that there do come times when, even understanding the goodness of God in this sense, it is still not easy to believe. That is when it is the duty of faith, grounded as it is on sure foundations, to set aside the many things about which there can be legitimate doubts, and to hold fast the basic Christian belief in a good God.

> I see the wrong that round me lies,
>   I feel the guilt within;
> I hear, with groan and travail-cries,
>   The world confess its sin.
>
> Yet, in the maddening maze of things,
>   And tossed by storm and flood,
> To one fixed trust my spirit clings:
>   I know that God is good!

How do we know? What are the sure foundations for this belief? Do we deduce it from a study of Nature? Do we see it in the state of man's relationship with his neighbours? Can it be traced in any of the ancient historic religions? Are we just guessing, and perhaps making a problem out of nothing? Are we speculating or gambling against the evidence when we say we believe in the existence of a supreme Being whom we can address in prayer without blasphemy as 'Good God'? Is it obscurantism or cant to be a man

> Who trusted God was love indeed
>   And love Creation's final law,
> Tho' Nature, red in tooth and claw
>   With ravine, shriek'd against his creed?

The fact is that we Christians are sure that God is good not because we have seen signs of it in the world around us, but because He has told us so Himself. This truth was first made known to mankind through the ministry of the prophets, priests and psalmists of the Old Testament, and later even more clearly in the New. For instance, in the robust atmosphere of the Psalms, when times were hard and devout men of God had a struggle to find a faith, and then had to cling to it against many odds, they show a firm belief in the righteousness of God. There was never a shadow of doubt in a devout Hebrew's mind that his God was just—however appearances might seem to disclaim it. Faced by the prosperity of the wicked and the sufferings of the innocent, there were times, certainly, when they cried out 'O God, why?' and 'O God, how long?' (see Pss. xiii. 1, 2, lxxiv. 1, 10, lxxix. 5, xciv. 3). But no delay in answers to prayer, no mysterious inequality of success in this life, and no calamitous disasters seem to have shaken their strong faith that 'God is a righteous judge' (Ps. vii. 11); 'Good and upright is the Lord' (Ps. xxv. 8). 'O taste and see that the Lord is good! Happy is the man who takes refuge in him!' (Ps. xxxiv. 8). 'The Lord is good to all' (Ps. cxlv. 9).

We find the same theme of God's love and goodness repeatedly declared by the prophets. 'The Lord waits to be gracious to you; therefore he exalts himself to show mercy to you. For the Lord is a God of justice; . . . he will surely be gracious to you at the sound of your cry' (Is. xxx. 18, 19). 'The mountains may depart and the hills be removed, but my steadfast love shall not depart from you, . . . says the Lord, who has compassion on you' (Is. liv. 10). 'I led them with cords of compassion, with the bands of love, and I became to them as one who eases the yoke on their jaws, and I bent down to them and fed them' (Ho. xi. 4). 'Return to the Lord, your God, for he is gracious and merciful, slow to anger, and abounding in steadfast love' (Joel ii. 13). 'He does not retain his anger for ever because he delights in steadfast love' (Mi. vii. 18). 'The Lord is good, a stronghold in the day of trouble' (Na. i. 7). 'The Lord within her is righteous, he does no wrong; every morning he shows forth his justice, each dawn he does not fail' (Zp. iii. 5). So the refrain is carried on from one man's inspired lips to another. In all the vagaries and vicissitudes of their national life, the leaders of God's people retained a profound faith in the goodness of their God which nothing could shake.

This truth was, of course, confirmed and illustrated in the life of our Lord Himself. When Jesus was facing the crisis of His own sufferings, the testimony of those who had nothing to gain personally from their witness (and who therefore had no reason to falsify their verdict) converges in the gospel story to establish the fact of His, and therefore of God's, essential goodness. Judas, casting down on the temple floor the thirty despicable pieces of silver which bought Jesus' betrayal, cried out : 'I have betrayed innocent blood.' Pilate, who had reached the peak of his magisterial career without learning the meaning of truth, had to admit : 'I find no fault in this man.' Procula his wife, whose dreams had been disturbed by what she had heard of the wonder of Jesus' life, sent an urgent message to her husband to keep his hands off 'this just person'. The tortured criminal, who had been able to hear the Lord's words of forgiveness for His tormentors, witnessed to his unrepentant colleague that 'this man has done nothing wrong'. The Roman officer in charge of the guard echoed the same verdict as he watched Him die : 'Certainly this was a righteous man.' This combined evidence of those who were not His followers, supported as it is by that of those who lived closest to Him, presents to the world a figure of unique goodness, the embodiment on this earth of One who must be good too : God, His Father and ours.

This faith of ours in the goodness of God rests not only on the authority of what men thought of our Lord's own Person and life, but also equally on that of His own teaching. 'No one is good but God alone', Jesus said (Lk. xviii. 19) to the wealthy young man who approached Him as 'Good Teacher', thereby unconsciously attesting His divinity. 'I am the good shepherd,' Jesus claimed for Himself, the Shepherd Beautiful as the Greek here implies, good through and through in every characteristic, and in great winsomeness. The loving care of the kindly heavenly Father for His creatures is the theme of much of the Sermon on the Mount, and of many of our Lord's parables. The very notion of Father implies One who is willing to give us our daily bread and forgive us our daily trespasses. Jesus made it clear beyond all possible doubt that God is a God of love; a love which far exceeds all human affection (Mt. vii. 11); a love which loves the unlovely, right on to the end (Jn. xiii. 1); a love which took Him to the cross, the place whither He bore 'our griefs and carried our sorrows', so that 'with his stripes we are healed'. In the light of all this, no-one can really doubt the goodness of God. We have seen enough evidence here from the Bible to enable us, whatever doubts may sometimes assail us, to cling to the faith of our childhood, that we have a good and loving Father in heaven.

> The same old baffling questions! O my friend,
> I cannot answer them. In vain I send
> My soul into the dark, where never burn
> The lamps of science, nor the natural light
> Of Reason's sun and stars! I cannot learn
> Their great and solemn meanings, nor discern
> The awful secrets of the eyes which turn
> Evermore on us through the day and night!
>
> With silent challenge and a dumb demand,
> Proffering the riddles of the dread unknown,
> Like the calm Sphinxes, with their eyes of stone,
> Questioning the centuries from their veils of sand!
> I have no answer for myself or thee,
> Save that I learned beside my mother's knee;
> 'All is of God that is, and is to be;
> And God is good.' Let this suffice us still,
> Resting in childlike trust upon His will
> Who moves to His great ends unthwarted by the ill.

This last sentence of Whittier's noble poem brings us to consider the 'almightiness' of God. It was J. S. Mill's contention that one could not believe in God being at the same time both good and omnipotent. He is prepared to admit God's goodness (which is handsome of him), but he cannot accept His being all-powerful. 'The notion of a providential government by an omnipotent Being for the good of his creatures must be entirely dismissed.'[1] In other words, he denies the Christian belief in providence,

[1] J. S. Mill, *Essays*, p. 243.

that God does 'move to His great ends unthwarted by the ill'.

What is the biblical basis for asserting that the God, whom we have seen is undoubtedly declared to be good, is also almighty? There are many passages, of which we can look at a few. Away back at the beginning of civilization, for instance, we find declared the omnipotence and justice of the Lord, who introduced Himself to Abram with the words, 'I am God Almighty' (Gn. xvii. 1). It will be recalled how, later, on an occasion when the actions of God in judgment on Sodom might well call in question His love, Abraham, the man of a faith that did not rest on appearances, declared : 'Shall not the Judge of all the earth do right?' (Gn. xviii. 25). In this very same chapter, in the personal context of the conception by his wife Sarah of a son in her old age, the man of faith was challenged by his heavenly visitor with the words : 'Is anything too hard for the Lord?' (Gn. xviii. 14).

On the basis of these and many other passages in the Bible, as well as on the utter impossibility of imagining a semi-potent God, each member of the Christian Church, century after century, has declared to the world, 'I believe in God the Father Almighty.' By the phrase 'Father', we have already seen that we mean a God who is good, and just, and loving. What do we mean exactly by calling Him 'Almighty'? Some people who take pleasure in tying up Christians in argument, try to simplify the issue by asking : If God really is all-powerful why does He not intervene? Why does He not stretch out His hand and, in some dramatic or spectacular way, stop this piece of suffering, or that? They do not stop to think how logically it would follow that, if God were to do this, there would be no end to the need for His interference in human life. Every time I say something which will hurt someone else, God must strike me dumb. Every time a careless driver neglects his duty on the road, God must bring his car to an abrupt halt. Every time a husband leaves his wife and children to follow a paramour, God must appear in some way and forcibly frustrate that evil action. The unreasonableness of expecting the Creator to treat His creatures like that is obvious to anyone who appreciates the privilege of being a human being. The actions of almighty God, inspired as they always will be by love, and measured by justice, will never operate to make us less men than He has created us. We are not puppets to be moved about willy-nilly and disposed of as an inscrutable divine authority dictates, irrespective of our wishes. We have a freedom of choice and decision which is part of the dignity of the human race. But this ability to choose the good when it is offered, includes, inevitably, the power to choose the bad also. God's almightiness does not deprive us of this right. Rather it shows itself in other ways, such as dealing with us when we make the wrong choice, and overruling our circumstances when we have refused the promptings of our conscience.

However, the closeness of personal interest that exists between God and His children does lead many to believe that God will sometimes actually intervene in their affairs, and much Christian prayer is inspired by such a belief. Archbishop William Temple in one of his earlier works explains what he thinks about such 'particular providences'. 'To maintain spiritual contact with God produces, it would seem, a sensitiveness to the Divine Will which usually shows itself only in the actions which it prompts. Personally I believe that a similar result may be produced by intercession. When I prayed for the safety of my friends during the Great War, I did not suppose that God would deflect bullets to save them, but I did and do believe that He might see fit to prompt them to some "accidental" movement which would save them. The impulse to pray is justified if such a thing is even possible. But it remains true that even if there are instances of such intervention, they are rare. . . .'[1] Indeed, such mystical influencing of the action of His children by the divine Spirit can hardly be regarded as being the same as forcible intervention on the part of God, which would in many ways deprive a man of his power to choose and decide on his own initiative.

Kierkegaard, the great Danish philosopher, whose teachings are now being so widely appreciated in the Christian Church, was a man whose sufferings seem to have inspired much of his insight. Was he not right when he declared that the greatest good that can be done to

[1] *Christus Veritas*, p. 195.

anyone is to make him free, and only God's omnipotence
could endure the operation of that freedom? Free will includes the power, by neglect or deliberate ill will, to bring
hurt upon others. We cannot blame God for the sufferings
of humanity, when so large a part of them is due to the
wrongful exercise by us of that power to be good which
includes the liberty to be bad. The almighty love of God
has limited the sphere of His own direct operations to
include our freedom of choice. The fact that we do wrong
and bring suffering to others does not mean that God is
not almighty. It means that His almighty power must
operate in other ways, some of which we shall be seeing
later in this book. The fact, then, that the children do not
always behave as they should, that they quarrel and hurt
one another and themselves, is no argument against their
having a loving and just father who cares intensely for
their best welfare, and who is himself hurt when they
abuse their freedom. That, magnified on a divine scale, is
the Christian belief. It is in the assurance that there *is*
meaning in suffering that we write these lines. The world,
unenlightened by faith, and anxious to enjoy the sensuali-
ties and pleasures of life undisturbed, regards suffering
not only as without purpose, but as altogether evil. The
Christian, on the other hand, in the light of what he reads
in the Bible and experiences in his person, is essentially an
optimist; he sees trouble as far from meaningless, and to
him suffering can be a stepping-stone to a better life. This
he asserts, not in any glib spirit of cant, but with a real
sense of awe and humility. The Christian confidently
believes this because his loving Father has taught him so.
Rather than being in a hurry to know the answer to his
cries 'Why?' and 'How long?', he is content to stand with
the prophet Habakkuk on his watch-tower waiting to see
what God may have to say to him :

'O Lord, how long shall I cry for help, and thou wilt
not hear? Or cry to thee "Violence!" and thou wilt not
save? Why dost thou make me see wrongs and look upon
trouble? Destruction and violence are before me; strife
and contention arise. . . . Why dost thou look on faithless
men, and art silent when the wicked swallows up the man
more righteous than he? . . . I will take my stand to watch,
and station myself on the tower, and look forth to see

what he will say to me, and what I will answer concerning
my complaint.' When God has spoken to him, the prophet
reaches a sublimity of trust in the face of dire calamity
which should be the experience of every man whose faith
can wait for God's time. 'Though the fig tree do not blos-
som, nor fruit be on the vines, the produce of the olive fail
and the fields yield no food, the flock be cut off from the
fold and there be no herd in the stalls, yet I will rejoice in
the Lord, I will joy in the God of my salvation' (Hab. i. 2,
3, 13, ii. 1, iii. 17, 18).

CHAPTER II

ANSWERS OLD AND NEW

UNINVITED, unprepared for, and unexplained
trouble has never been a respecter of persons. The
uneven fall of calamity on innocent and guilty
alike has been a problem to thoughtful people from time
immemorial. It becomes, as we have seen, particularly
acute when there is a belief in a personal, loving God, but
even without this faith, man cries out for an explanation.
One of the best-known ancient answers to the problem of
pain is the Hindu doctrine of *Karma*, once rigidly believed
in by all Hindus and only now beginning to break down
under the enlightenment of modern education. *Karma*
means literally 'actions', and implies the result in life today
of one's activities in a previous existence. A man suffers
what he deserves to suffer, for he has brought it on himself. The lonely misery of the child-widow, the sightless
sufferings of the blind beggar, the enforced humiliation of
the outcaste, the hollow belly of the hungry—these are all,
in this view, the merited punishments of the sufferers, for
their misdeeds in a former life. If that life has been particularly bad (and to a Hindu this means not sin in the
Christian sense but behaviour not in accordance with
caste custom and so forth) the unfortunate soul will be
likely to reappear in the animal world. The Laws of
Manu, a codified system of Hindu customary belief dating
from about the fifth century BC, say, for instance, that

men who delight in doing hurt become carnivorous animals, those who eat forbidden food become worms; for stealing grain a man becomes a rat; for stealing milk, a cow; for stealing meat, a vulture, and for stealing vehicles, a camel.[1] Indian thought links this doctrine of *Karma* with that of the transmigration of souls, and, to the Hindu, the only real redemption is release from this endless cycle of birth and rebirth, a release which is promised to none, and hardly ever claimed by even the most earnest devotee. It is said that the average existence of any one soul is 84 *lakhs* (8,400,000) of rebirths, which is an Indian way of describing the practical impossibility of ever breaking away from the bonds of these spiritual wanderings, a prospect one of their poets bemoans in the words :

> How many births are past I cannot tell,
> How many yet to come no man can say,
> But this alone I know, and know full well,
> That pain and grief embitter all the way.

While this tedious necessity of the soul's being born again and again may well appear a forlorn prospect, it must be acknowledged that the concept of suffering in this world being exactly measured by the guilt incurred previously, does provide some sort of answer to the question 'Why?' The Hindu believes there is no injustice anywhere in life. As the rope trails behind the wandering bullock so our evil deeds inexorably follow us. We reap what we sow.

> Our acts our angels are, or good or ill,
> Our fatal shadows that walk by us still.

In a sense, of course, this is true. But, unfortunately, we also reap what others have sown, and we pass on to others the fruits of our own sowing. The intensely individualistic outlook which parcels each one of us up separately and says that each person's pains are entirely and only due to the misbehaviour of that person's soul when it was in some other person's body, actually creates more problems than it solves. We can, for example, inquire how the souls which have taken up their residence in an animal have any chance, by good behaviour, of earning a better, even a human, existence again. What does a good rat do for a

[1] Quoted by S. Cave, *Redemption, Hindu and Christian*, p. 188.

living? Are there any bad worms? Does a good flea only
bite dogs, and a bad flea bite human beings? Alternatively,
we could pose an arithmetical puzzle which makes belief
in reincarnation somewhat formidable. Granted that
every soul alive today in any living creature was something or someone else previously, and so on back to the
earliest days of human history, how can one account for
an increase of population down the years from the
primaeval beginnings? If life began with fewer souls than
exist today, where have the extra ones come from? Do
souls have fissional capabilities?

But these more fruitless questions must not obscure the
real seriousness of the subject. Millions of people are still
held in the grip of this hope which is no hope, this explanation of the justice of the universe, which, on examination, proves to be gross injustice. For how can it be
called fair that I should suffer today for something I cannot remember having done wrong? In the greatest of the
Hindu classics, the *Bhagavad Gita* (4.5), only the god
Krishna himself can remember his former existence, and
after all he is a god. Souls have no memories. Memory is
a faculty linked with our physical bodies, and it has yet
to be proved that anyone can recall the virtues or vices of
their previous existence (supposing they had one) which
explains their predicament today. What kind of a god is
it that punishes people for something they do not know,
and for which they can neither apologize nor repent?

For the Christian, the matter is one which is finally
settled on the authority of Christ Himself. Belief in reincarnation appears to have existed in the New Testament
era, for we find the disciples asking Jesus if a man who
had been born blind was by any chance so suffering for
his sins, which of course must have been committed in a
previous existence (Jn. ix. 2, 3). Jesus quite definitely
denies this, and as there is no other passage in the Bible
which deals with this oriental belief, which Theosophists
like Mrs. Besant have tried to popularize in the Western
world, the Christian believer looks elsewhere for his
explanation of pain.

Buddhism is a religion of which the very origin was a
revolt against suffering. The Buddha himself lived the
sheltered life of a wealthy young man until a certain day

when, the story goes, he was brought face to face with an old man, a sick man, and a dead man. This set him thinking about his own inevitable decay, and at first for entirely selfish and personal reasons he began to seek a way of deliverance. Born a Hindu he naturally inherited belief in the law of *Karma* and accepted himself as bound like everyone else to the revolving wheel of repeated existences. Until the moment of his 'Awakening' he found that neither yoga nor asceticism, both of which he practised assiduously, promised any release. Enlightenment is said to have come to him eventually as he was meditating under a fig tree, when he saw what he called the Four Great Truths—

I Birth is sorrow, age is sorrow, sickness is sorrow, death is sorrow, clinging to earthly things is sorrow.

II Birth and re-birth, the chain of reincarnation, result from the thirst for life together with passion and desire.

III The only escape from this thirst is the annihilation of desire.

IV The only way of escape from this thirst is by following the Eightfold Path; right belief, right resolve, right word, right act, right life, right effort, right thinking, right meditation.[1]

Nirvana to the Buddhist is this extinction of desire. The word literally means 'blowing-out', like the snuffing of a candle. Only by the cutting off of existence can desire be killed, for desire is the root cause of all suffering. Buddha taught that if one strictly followed the eightfold path of right conduct there might be an outside chance of bringing one's *Karma* to an end. This meant, in an existence not too remote, attaining the necessary self-annihilation, when the personality 'drops like the glistening dew into the silver sea'.

The inadequacy of this explanation of suffering is obvious at once. As Stanley Jones points out, it is a case of 'Get rid of your headache by cutting off your head'.[2] To the Christian, the personality is a sacred thing. We are characters whom God has created, each of us with an

---

[1] E. W. Hopkins, *Religions of India*, p. 305.
[2] *Christ and Human Suffering*, p. 53

infinite variety of appearance, characteristics and temperaments. We are individuals whom God loves one by one, as Jesus pointed out in the parables of the lost coin, the lost sheep, and the lost son. We are men and women for whom Christ died so that our personalities might be set free from the bonds of evil and be given the strength not to dodge trouble, but to rise above it. Buddhism is escapism *par excellence*. Not believing in any kind of personal God, the Buddha could not of course be expected to anticipate the Christian belief in a personal relationship between the soul and its Saviour, a relationship forged in the troubles of this world and fulfilled in the bliss of the world to come. Nor could anything he taught reach the heights of the followers of the suffering Servant foretold in Isaiah when they actually welcome pain as a means of strengthening that personal relationship with God. Far from praying to escape, or hoping to cease to exist, the Christian is fundamentally an optimist who cannot follow the Buddha's logic. He sees this world, in spite of all the troubles its flesh is heir to, as the arena in which battle is joined with evil, and all thought of retreat is brushed aside by the determination to conquer.

When we come to look at the religion of Islam we find again some kind of an explanation provided to the question, Why suffering? The overriding Muslim belief is the altogether otherness of the one God, Allah. He may call himself the 'All-Merciful', along with his ninety-eight other names, but the chief characteristic of the god which Muhammed his 'prophet' proclaimed, is of his inexorable *will*. The will of God is not something to be prayed for or sought after as the Christian envisages it. It is something which, come what may, do what we like, inevitably happens. *Allah katib*, God has willed it, is the answer given to the mother mourning her child, the frustrated lover, the cancer-ridden patient or the bankrupt householder. 'By no means', says the Koran, 'can aught befall us save what Allah has destined for us.' [1] What we are, what we do, what happens to us—all these things are decreed by God. All evil comes from him, as he shall choose. Men prosper and flourish or suffer and perish, as

[1] Surah 9.51.

the inscrutable deity has proposed, and no questions may be asked. 'God misleadeth whom he will and whom he will he guideth', says the Koran.[1]

This being so, there is only one attitude a true Muslim can take when faced with calamity. He has to submit. 'Islam' means 'submission'. A grim unquestioning fatalism is inevitable with such a rigid idea of God. The sufferer must take it like a man. We must face it, as the Stoics used to teach, with the courage of an athlete who uses opposition as a means to strengthen his muscles.

> In the fell clutch of circumstance,
> I have not winced nor cried aloud :
> Under the bludgeonings of chance
> My head is bloody, but unbowed.

Many people, even in Christian lands, might say in this unenlightened generation that that is still a fine attitude to take. We are urged to keep a stiff upper lip, not to complain or seek the sympathy of others, to carry our sorrows alone and make the best we can of things. Of course one cannot but admire what this spartan outlook implies, but we shall see, as we pursue the subject further, that while the humanist can hardly expect to rise higher than this, the Christian certainly can and should.

In any case, with the Bible open before us, nothing can convince us that the Muslim idea of God has anything in common with the picture Jesus gave the world, of a heavenly Father who cares for the fallen sparrow, who raises the fallen woman, whose ears are open to the cries of all in distress. The Son of God, we remember, spent the greater part of His ministry in the healing of the sick and the relief of suffering. From Him and His work we learn that God is a God who cares. There is nothing of Thomas Hardy's 'President of the Immortals finishing his sport with Tess', in the New Testament picture of God the Father. We shall be thinking later of the fellow-feeling in our pains which Jesus displayed. Meanwhile we must firmly reject the sub-Christian view of God which demands of the sufferer an attitude of mere submission to a fate without meaning or purpose, for we believe that we live in a God-cared-for world, and that love reigns in the heart of the Eternal.

[1] Surah 14.4.

From the Muslim or modern Stoic attitude to suffering, let us turn to its opposite, the Epicurean, for like the others it has many followers today. This, though in a different way from Buddhism, is also an escapist philosophy, if we can honour it with such a name. Suffering cannot be avoided, Epicureans argue. It had better be drowned: Eat, drink and be as merry as we can under the circumstances, for tomorrow we shall probably snuff out. Again and again in cases of bereavement or sudden disaster, well-meaning neighbours come in with the only remedy they can think of, 'Have a drink, old boy. You'll feel better afterwards.' Ready recourse to liquor to try to drown trouble in an artificial sense of well-being, or to obscure it in a haze of confused emotions, may not rank as a philosophy, but it is an extremely common form of 'comfort'. Perhaps it is unkind to condemn it without paying tribute to the genuine goodwill which so often lies behind such advice. Undoubtedly a degree of fictitious courage can be stimulated in this way to carry an individual through the crisis of some terrible experience. But the aftermath leaves a vacuity which the Eastern alcoholic knew so well, when he cried for

> Another and another Cup to drown
> The Memory of this Impertinence!

and many men and women regret the day when trouble led them into the grip of alcoholism which they now find they cannot break off.

It is not, of course, only to drink that people turn in their troubles. Some will seek distraction in the gay company of others, hoping not to be left alone long enough to think, fearing to face their problems by themselves because they know they are without an answer to them. Others, in uneasiness at the suffering which follows their thoughtless actions, will try to make nothing of it, and, like T. S. Eliot's parody of Oliver Goldsmith's young lady, will seek a more modern form of solace.

> When lovely woman stoops to folly, and
> Paces about her room again, alone,
> She smoothes her hair with automatic hand,
> And puts a record on the gramophone.

Modern hedonism is so desperate when it comes up against anything that takes the pleasure out of pleasure-seeking, that it can only think of rushing its devotees faster and faster along the road of trouble in the hope that they will not notice what they are passing through, so keenly do they press on to the hoped-for happy ending. But the superficiality of such euphoria as drink or gaiety can produce, leaves a disillusionment afterwards which can drive its victims still further away from the spiritual help which they could find if they looked in God's direction. Those who adopt a shallow attitude to life like this are invariably unprepared for any break-up of their happiness, such as bereavement, loss or pain. Caught unawares, they desperately pretend to themselves that the grief is not as bad as it really is, and all will come right in the end. But they still find the ghost of their trouble reappearing at every sober moment, still demanding to be dealt with.

Before we leave these non-Christian explanations of suffering, a word or two must be said about the modern phenomenon of Christian Science. This is not the place to make a full examination of this American nineteenth-century panacea for pain. This has been well done in several books.[1] We are simply interested in its inadequacy as an answer to the problem of suffering. Dr. André Schlemmer condemns the movement categorically, on the grounds that, 'all the confused hotchpotch of extravagant arguments contained in the book which serves as a second Bible for the Christian Scientist (*Science and Health, with Key to the Scriptures* by Mary Baker Eddy) has nothing in common with either scientific construction, or with the content of Scripture . . . It is an optimistic American transposition of Buddhist conceptions.'[2] Dr. Weatherhead sees some good in this strange perversion of undoubted truth, but, as we shall see shortly, he also points out the fact that this religion cannot really claim to be either Christian or scientific.

The Christian Scientist asks us to extend our credulity to breaking-point. In believing that God is all, God is good, and God is Spirit one might assume that there is room for orthodoxy. But Mrs. Eddy, out of whose own neurotic mind arose strange metaphysical ramblings,

[1] Particularly: Weatherhead, *Psychology, Religion and Healing*.

[2] *Faith and Medicine*, p. 16.

taught that only Mind (or Spirit) is real. Matter, as the Hindus or Buddhists would agree, is *Maya*, illusion, which means that sin, evil and disease are unreal. 'It's all in the mind you know', to quote our modern Goons, would sum up the basic belief of Christian Science. 'Science shows that what is termed "matter" is but the subjective state of what is termed by the author "mortal mind".' [1] Health of body can be obtained, Mrs. Eddy claimed, when one is convinced that illness and pain are a figment of the imagination. The author does not seem to have been unduly disturbed by the inconsistency of what she proclaimed with the obvious facts of ordinary experience. When she goes as far as to say, 'A boil simply manifests, through inflammation and swelling, a belief in pain, and this belief is called a boil', we wonder that anyone can believe her, and have reason to think that Job would have had quite a lot to say to her on this rather sore subject. We are reminded of the oft-quoted limerick :

> There was a faith-healer of Deal
> Who said that though pain is not real
> When I sit on a pin
> And it punctures my skin
> I dislike what I fancy I feel.

But it is important to be fair, and we must acknowledge that Christian Science emphasizes a most important aspect of truth, which the Christian Church and the medical profession are at last beginning to teach again, the power of the mind over the body. More will be said about this when we come to look at faith-healing, and notice the interplay of mental and physical processes on each other. Christian Scientists, of course, are by no means the only people who draw attention to the curative effect on the body of right attitudes of the mind. We read these days of the gospel of Positive Thinking. Without regarding it as in any way a cure for sin or the end-all of religious experience, we must honestly admit the immense value in the relief of suffering of the optimism of this kind of outlook. Its emphasis on the importance of hope, trust and courage, as health-giving attitudes, is most valuable. Its manner of driving out fear by a hope based on false premises may be theo-

[1] *Science and Health*, p. 114.

logically unsound, but practically it is indeed an ally to the healing processes of nature.

But when we have said this, the Christian is still convinced that Christian Science holds no real answer to the problem associated with pain and suffering, for a number of reasons. In the first place, because it is wrong to make the health of the body pre-eminent, and to treat God as a means to this end. Other faith-healers than Christian Scientists come near to making this mistake, though they would probably never admit it. But in Christian Science, physical health, even though based on the denial of its opposite, is raised to the position of the supreme good, and the glory of God hardly enters into the picture at all.

Secondly, the Christian cannot accept the belief that the body is unreal and outside the scheme of divine redemption. He believes that our bodies are to be presented to God as a living sacrifice (Rom. xii. 1); that they are the very temple of God's Spirit (1 Cor. vi. 19); and that they are to be transformed at the resurrection, but still to be our own recognizable selves (1 Cor. xv. 44, 51–54). The Christian will feel that if the matter of the body is an illusion then the coming of Christ, when He was 'made flesh' and dwelt among us (Jn. i. 14), could not have been real either. To accept this is asking too much of any Christian who believes the creed of the Christian Church, which since the fourth century AD has declared : 'Jesus Christ, . . . being of one substance with the Father, . . . who for us men, and for our salvation came down from heaven, and was incarnate by the Holy Ghost of the Virgin Mary, and was made man.'

Thirdly, Mrs. Eddy would ignore the next phrase of the Nicene Creed, 'He suffered under Pontius Pilate.' The sufferings of Christ, like those of human beings, did not really take place; nor was there any reality in the pains of those He sought to heal. Jesus was deluded in these matters (and therefore in others too). Mrs. Eddy goes so far as to say, 'Had wisdom characterized all his sayings, he would not have prophesied his own death and thereby hastened or caused it.' A Christian who values the New Testament as a true and faithful account of the life and teaching of Jesus recorded by those who knew Him best and who had nothing to gain by falsifying their account, will not be persuaded that the contumely, shame, agony and cruelty which Jesus endured were unreal, or that the death that these sufferings led up to was unnecessary. The Christian Scientist, of course, does not believe in sin as any more real than any other evil, and therefore he sees no redemptive purpose in Christ's becoming incarnate and dying and rising again. It is no answer to the problem of evil to be told that the Saviour came needlessly into an unreal world to save it from sins that have no objective existence. We must, therefore, discard this modern religious explanation together with its contemporary and ancient counterparts as we try to find some satisfaction in our struggle with the problems to which evil and pain give rise.

CHAPTER III

DIVINE JUDGMENT

JOHN STUART MILL, who as we have already seen was deeply exercised by the problem of evil, showed surprising lack of depth in his argument that justice demands an exact relation between man's sins and his sufferings. If the world were a community of islands each with its Robinson Crusoe in solitary isolation upon it, it might be thought possible that he should bear the result of his own misdemeanours on his own head—but this would mean including as scrupulously fair, for instance, any dysentery that he might get through ignorance of what he could or could not safely eat. Would that be just? Again, if he were to get rheumatism or pneumonia through the vagaries of the climate, would he be to blame? Can Mill's argument be accepted even on the basis of such a quite unrealistic picture of man as an individual, without any neighbours or forefathers? Science tells us of the immense influence of heredity on a man's life and temperament. Sociology emphasizes the vital importance of environment, and reminds us that we are all tied up in the bundle of life together. The Bible leaves us in no doubt that God created the human race not as a collection of isolated units but as a great family, in which, if one member suffers, the other members suffer with it.

However, there are still many tortured people who ask themselves, or more likely ask their doctor or minister, if their illness, it may be, or their tragedy, is a punishment for their sins. At least one of Job's so-called 'comforters' held the opinion that suffering was always a consequence of sin. 'Think now,' says Eliphaz, 'who that was innocent ever perished? Or where were the upright cut off? As I have seen, those who plough iniquity and sow trouble reap the same' (iv. 7, 8). Not a few say resignedly with a sigh, 'I suppose I have deserved this.' They probably do not really believe it, but for want of a better explanation and in deference to a popularly-held belief, they take the blame on themselves, though often with an implied insinuation that there is something unfair about it all. If their friends were to agree with them and say sincerely that the sickness or accident they are suffering from is a direct consequence of some sin of theirs, they would be most indignant—and who will blame them? It is heart-breaking for a man already bowed down in trouble, to be told that he is to blame for his agony. That kind of insensitive accusation can almost break the courage of the sufferer, and it is by no means always true.

It is impossible to prove in every case a close and specific connection between what a man undergoes in suffering and what he has done in sin, though undoubtedly there is sometimes such a link. The problem is made more difficult by the suggestion that, if I suffer for my misdeeds, the punishment *exactly* fits the crime. To be fair it should be so. If it does not do so, then how can it be fair? It may be too harsh or too lenient, in which case there is no longer real justice. Zophar considered that, great as Job's sufferings obviously were, 'God exacts of you less than your guilt deserves' (xi. 6). When pinned down to the instance of the person of Job himself, who, we are told, was 'a perfect and an upright man', these words seem at first particularly cruel. But when we consider the horror of sin in general, and then realize that we are all sinners in various ways and degrees, it is hard to escape the fact that Zophar was right : in His mercy, God does not actually punish us according to our deserts, or we should be constant and terrible sufferers indeed. If we were to suffer in proportion to our wickedness, how could we ever be free from trouble, for sin is a very wide term, and does a day pass without our committing it, and thereby deserving the immediate judgment of God?

To get a balanced picture of this problem it will be worth while studying some of the instances recorded in the Bible where God is shown to be allowing divine punishment to take the form of pain or sickness, when 'whatever a man sows, that he will also reap' (Gal. vi. 7). We shall also see those passages which declare that no connection of cause and effect can be claimed in every instance of suffering. We can only take a selection of examples. The subject is really so large that it deserves much fuller treatment.

In the Old Testament era, before it was disclosed to the world that divine retribution is mainly reserved to the next life, and that deliverance from such judgment lies in the cross of Christ, it was frequently, though by no means invariably, taught that one suffered pain and even death at the hands of God in return for one's misdeeds. In the book of Numbers, for example, we are told that Miriam was struck down with a temporary attack of leprosy for questioning the behaviour and authority of her brother Moses, God's appointed leader and servant (xii). It appears that Moses' wife Zipporah had died and he had recently married an African woman which was not contrary to Jewish law, but which had offended his sister's and his brother Aaron's race prejudice and caused them to challenge his leadership. The dramatic onset of Miriam's leprosy was immediately understood by them both as a judgment of God and she was only cured in answer to the impassioned praying of Moses himself.

In the book of Deuteronomy we read of Moses being punished on account of his failure to restrain the people of Israel, and for not rising to his responsibility as leader for upholding the holiness of God (xxxii. 50, 51). With him the punishment was to die while he was still in good health (xxxiv. 7), and not to enjoy the experience of his followers in the land of milk and honey to which he had led them. This may seem to a modern reader an excessively harsh judgment, but it is worth noting that, to Moses, death was no enemy for 'the Lord knew (him) face to face' (xxxiv. 10). Actually the last thing he did was to sing a song of praise to the God who 'loved his people' and whose justice he never personally questioned.

The story of David's adultery with Uriah's wife Bathsheba and his subsequent organizing of the death of Uriah ends on a clear note of immediate retribution. The prophet Nathan faces the king of Israel with his sin. David acknowledges it frankly and the prophet assures him of God's readiness to forgive him. But he then goes on to say that, though forgiven, justice demanded that the public should see clearly that there was no favouritism in kings' palaces and sin does not pay. The child of the adulterous union must die, and, in spite of the earnest prayers of the father, the child did die (2 Sa. xii. 7–18).

Another Old Testament instance of the judgment of God falling immediately on a man's sin, was when Gehazi the servant of Elisha the prophet deceived the Syrian captain Naaman, and secured for himself a useful haul of presents to which he was not entitled. At the word of the prophet, he suddenly succumbed to the leprosy of which Naaman had been cured, and there is no hint that he repented or recovered (2 Ki. v. 20–27).

When we come to the great prophets of Israel, we find that Jeremiah and Ezekiel, preaching at the time of the decay and obliteration of Israel as a nation, with all the calamities associated with that upheaval, tried to bring their people back to repentance by emphasizing that however tempting it is—after the fashion of a popular proverb —to lay all the blame for one's sufferings on the sins of one's forbears, one must bear a great measure of responsibility oneself. 'In those days they shall no longer say: "The fathers have eaten sour grapes, and the children's teeth are set on edge." But every one shall die for his own sin; each man who eats sour grapes, his teeth shall be set on edge' (Je. xxxi. 29, 30). We find the same theme in one of Ezekiel's prophecies : 'What do you mean by repeating this proverb concerning the land of Israel, "The fathers have eaten sour grapes, and the children's teeth are set on edge"? As I live, says the Lord God, this proverb shall no more be used by you in Israel. Behold, all souls are mine; the soul of the father as well as the soul of the son is mine : the soul that sins shall die' (Ezk. xviii. 2–4).

It appears from these various quotations that in the period of the Old Testament, men of God were used from time to time to bring home to those who should have known better, particularly to the religious leaders, that they must expect to pay for their sins by a degree of suffering, even though those sins were forgiven by God. This truth was a safeguard against the inclination many would have, as they still do, to shuffle off the blame for their wrong-doing on to the shoulders of others. But at the same time it is quite clear that there is not, in the pre-Christian era, any such clearly-defined association between sin and suffering that would enable anyone to say that all my troubles are due to my sins, or that all my sins will lead to trouble. In the Old Testament, individual retribution is an occasional and perhaps rare occurrence. We are not told anywhere that punishment in the way of suffering *invariably* follows misdoing. Indeed, when it did do so it seems to have been made quite clear to the wrongdoer what was happening. But it was not by any means every sinner who was so punished. When Bildad, in the course of his so-called comforting of Job, suggested that the sudden death of his children was due to their sins, his words carry no strong conviction, for it does not appear to be God who is speaking at all (Jb. viii. 4). Bildad is simply repeating a popularly-held view, in the same way as the woman of Zarephath assumed that her son's severe illness was a judgment on her sins (1 Ki. xvii. 18).

When we come to look at the New Testament we again find certain marked instances of individual judgment following particular sins. Luke records the way in which the priest Zacharias, a most godly man, was struck dumb for nine months because he did not readily believe the announcement of the angel Gabriel that he and his wife Elizabeth would have a son in their old age (Lk. i. 6–20). The book of Acts records instances of even severer punishments. Ananias and Sapphira both fell dead for selling some property and bringing an offering of part of the proceeds to God and pretending it was all they got in the transaction (v. 1–11). Herod the king came to a gruesome and sudden end for allowing the populace to worship him with divine honours which neither his position nor his character could in any way warrant (xii. 23). Elymas the magician was overcome with blindness because he used his arts to frustrate the preaching of Barnabas and Paul (xiii. 10, 11). Paul, in his letter to the Corinthian church, suggests that some of their members are ill and have possibly died on account of their careless and callous attitude to the sacrament of Holy Communion (1 Cor. xi. 30).

These examples from periods of the sacred record, both before and after Christ, make it impossible for us to deny that even today there may be an element of retribution in our pains. But we can be certain of this, on the authority of our Lord Himself, that it is not always so. In the case of the man who had been blind from birth, He was asked, as we have seen, if by any chance this was due, not only to his own sins in a previous life, but also, possibly, to the sins of his parents. It is well known that certain forms of venereal disease do not infrequently result in the birth of blind children, when the innocent little ones most obviously do suffer for the sins of their parents. But on this occasion that was not the cause, and Jesus declared categorically that that wretched man's handicap could not be so easily explained away (Jn. ix. 3). Similarly, He quoted the instance when Pilate apparently ruthlessly exterminated certain rioting Galileans by slaughtering them in the temple precincts. Jesus says that those who died were not greater sinners than those who escaped. Similarly, in the instance when a great tower fell and killed eighteen persons, He says clearly that that was in no way a punishment on them for their sins. Jesus did, however, say: 'Unless you repent you will all likewise perish.' It would be fascinating to know the rest of what He said on this occasion, how He went on to develop this theme, with its apparently contradictory corollary. Perhaps He pointed out how the existence of Palestine as enemy-occupied territory, under the heel of a Roman dictator who would not stop at violent executions on the slightest provocation, was really the fruit of the nation's failure to fulfil its covenant with God. Again, possibly Jesus had something to say about the shoddy workmanship and neglected supervision which led to the collapse of that tower, sins, both of these, leading to disaster for the innocent sufferers.

Whatever the sacred Scriptures hide from us, we can at least learn that it is never right, with our very limited understanding of the meaning of suffering and our smaller understanding of the ways of divine providence, to assert dogmatically in the case of our own or anyone else's troubles that they are the due reward of their misdeeds. They may be; but it seems, from the biblical examples we have just looked at, that if this was so the sufferer was never left in any doubt when his trouble was a punishment. In many cases, the guilty ones were warned of what was coming to them, and sometimes they even took the risk and had only themselves to blame when the mills of God ground them slowly to dust. In other instances, such as when Nathan called on David, the sinner quietly accepted God's judgment as eminently fair. If it is true that, in the Bible, whenever an individual was being punished by God and that punishment took the form of tragedy or trouble, there was never any doubt about it, so it may still be today. There may be certain occasions in people's lives when the Almighty allows, or even ordains, pain as a punishment fit for their crime, but these are likely to be as rare today as they were in ancient times. Therefore, without morbidly digging in the muck-heap of past sin to try to trace a logical connection between that and its retribution, we ought, when we are called upon to suffer, to search our hearts and solemnly ask God to make it clear whether, in truth, our pain may not be God's way of rousing us to repentance.

When Jesus said, in the context we have already noticed, 'Unless you repent you will all likewise perish', He may have been giving a general warning that the neglect of God and His laws, and a refusal to repent, will certainly bring retribution of one kind or another. This is particularly true when we realize that while God cares for us and deals with us as individual persons, this is by no means to the exclusion of His dealings with us in community. It is when we come to think about this collective aspect of human trouble that some light falls on the particular problem of the suffering of the innocent. In the time of the prophet Ezekiel, for example, many people cried out to him in complaint, 'The way of the Lord is not just' (xviii. 25). God is not fair : to which God replied through His servant, 'Is my way not just? Is it not your ways that are not just?' We do not want to belittle the awful problem that arises in every thoughtful person's mind when faced by the sufferings, for instance, of children who on no account can be held in any way responsible for them; such things cannot be accounted for on personal grounds. Only in the smallest degree can a child suffer for its own misdeeds. But when we bear in mind the immensely formative powers of environment and heredity on the life and experience of children, we have entered the field where the principle of solidarity operates. Quite simply this means that it is impossible in human life to isolate the errors of one man from its effects upon another or upon many others. Most of the good things of life which we enjoy are due to the efforts of our predecessors or neighbours under the providential hand of God. The Almighty has created the human race in such a way that we are all interdependent, both for good and ill. But if we help one another sometimes, we hinder at other times. The tragedy is, that

> The evil that men do lives after them,
> The good is oft interred with their bones.

This principle of the continued suffering in after ages, due to the solidarity of humanity, can be seen clearly stated in the Bible. The classic expression of it is incorporated in the Decalogue where the Lord God is spoken of as 'visiting the iniquity of the fathers upon the children to the third and the fourth generation of those who hate me' (Ex. xx. 5). It is repeated in a further passage, 'The Lord . . . will by no means clear the guilty, visiting the iniquity of the fathers upon the children and the children's children, to the third and the fourth generation' (Ex. xxxiv. 6, 7). As critics of the Bible often fasten on these passages as portraying a God who has little relation to the God whom Jesus told the world was a loving heavenly Father, it is necessary to dwell on this at some length.

In the first place, let us remember that the idea that God is love is not confined to the New Testament. There were many scattered glimpses of this, long before God's love became incarnate in the Person of Jesus. Note that in the very passage quoted above, the mercy of God is the predominant theme : 'The Lord God, merciful and gracious, longsuffering, and abundant in goodness and truth, keeping mercy for thousands, forgiving iniquity and transgression and sin' (Ex. xxxiv. 6, 7, AV). A similar insight into the loving nature of God occurs in the book Deuteronomy, 'It was not because you were more in number than any other people that the Lord set his love upon you and chose you, for you were the fewest of all peoples; but it is because the Lord loves you' (vii. 7, 8). In the second part of the prophetic book Isaiah, we read of the divine care which had surrounded God's people through their long history. 'In all their affliction he was afflicted, and the angel of his presence saved them; in his love and in his pity he redeemed them' (lxiii. 9). Hosea describes God's willingness to welcome the returning and repentant Israel with the words : 'I will love them freely' (xiv. 4). The prophet Jeremiah also proclaimed the love of God in words which have brought comfort to thousands ever since he uttered them, 'I have loved you with an everlasting love; therefore I have continued my faithfulness to you' (xxxi. 3).

Furthermore, it is important to notice how in this very commandment, one which in some ways appears to present a harsh picture of the Lord God, the predominant feature is His Mercy. He shows 'mercy unto thousands (of generations) of them that love me, and keep my commandments'. The reading 'thousands of generations' is justified on the grounds of its parallel in the book of Deuteronomy—'Know therefore that the Lord thy God, he is God, the faithful God, which keepeth covenant and mercy with them that love him and keep his commandments to a thousand generations' (Ex. xx. 6; Dt. vii. 9, AV). Historically, it will be a very long time before it can be said that a thousand generations have come and gone. At an average of thirty years for one generation, there yet remain many more eons of recorded human history during which we are assured that the Lord's mercy is on those who respect Him. The phrase, of course, is a figure of speech. The emphasis in this context is not so much upon the outworking of divine retribution, as upon the amazing extent of divine mercy : endless, limitless, without respect of persons or measurement of sin. The God of the Old Testament is thus already portrayed in the earliest period of divine revelation as One who will forgive the sins of any who are willing to acknowledge His claims, and, in the words of C. S. Lewis, 'tread Adam's dance backward' and repent.

But, at the same time, it is impossible to ignore the other half of the second commandment. We must not attribute human passions to God, and on no account read the words, He visits the sins 'of the fathers upon the children . . .' as displaying the spirit of a human parent who has lost his temper and is taking vengeance on the innocent. What is implied here is the principle which we have already seen, that God has so ordered human life that if one generation sows dragons' teeth, the subsequent one will find them growing up into a horrifying horde of ruined homes, squalid slums, homeless refugees, motherless orphans and fretting captives. These are the direct fruit of the intransigence and pride of those who can settle their national differences only by armed conflict, or who go their own way, ignoring their duties to their neighbours. The child whose parents have selfishly allowed their differences to develop into divorce, finds itself insecure in an unloving world, and before long becomes a problem to his teacher, or a delinquent in the courts, not on account of his own wrong-doing, but because of the sins of his parents. Dr. Leslie Weatherhead in his book on this whole subject gives instances of how, in the earthquakes at San Francisco and Quetta, many lost their possessions and their lives because of negligent building and the irresponsible neglect of rudimentary precautions.[1]

In these, and in thousands of similar cases, the sufferings of so many cannot be held as an argument against the justice of God. They are rather a demonstration of the continued spread of evil's influence in the world, like the ripples of a pond disturbed by a stone thrown upon it. God cannot be held responsible for man's inhumanity to man. In His providential love for man, He has made him as capable of doing right as of doing wrong. But when a

[1] *Why do Men Suffer?*, p. 106.

man misuses his free-will, the sinner himself must take the blame; a blame all the heavier because the results of his sin fall so often on innocent heads. It is important, however, to note that in this commandment, which warns of the consequences of sin on future generations, there is a definite limit beyond which the effect of sin seems to work itself out: the ripples gradually die away, in the scriptural phrase, after 'the third or fourth generation'. Countries do gradually recover from the devastation of war. Children are not noticeably suffering from the failings of their great-grandparents. The outworkings of sin are strictly limited like this, while the outgoing of God's love and mercy knows no limits whatever.

To sum up what we have seen so far, let us listen to the heart cry of the displaced persons in Babylon, whose Lamentations form so pathetically beautiful a part of the Bible. For two generations they have been undergoing slave-labour under the heel of a dictator régime, in a captivity which has almost, but not quite, succeeded in extinguishing their one true faith in God. The author of these Lamentations, thought by some to be Jeremiah, has expressed their misery and their faith in five immortal chapters. This collection of poems, which were probably composed towards the end of the sixth century, tells of the accumulation of the people's troubles. Their treasured city, Jerusalem, had been razed to the ground, with all the hopes it enshrined laid in dust also. Vast numbers of the people were living in slave conditions in Babylon, while those, including the prophet Jeremiah, who were not amongst the captives, were enduring enemy occupation in what had once been their own dear country. The miseries of famine were added to their losses through pillage and war. Public worship, which had maintained their morale as the general conditions of the nation had gradually worsened, had now been brought to an end. The prophet recognized all these troubles as the fruit of his people's sin, and urged them to repent and accept the chastening hand of the Lord. 'How lonely sits the city that was full of people! How like a widow has she become . . . The roads to Zion mourn, for none come to the appointed feasts . . . Her foes have become the head, her enemies prosper, because the Lord has made her suffer for

the multitude of her transgressions . . .' (i. 1, 4, 5). So cries
the stricken Jerusalem, and then she goes on to call on
those who see her in distress to recognize in it the fierceness of God's wrath; 'Is it nothing to you, all you who
pass by? Look and see if there is any sorrow like my sorrow
which was brought upon me, which the Lord inflicted on
the day of his fierce anger . . . My transgressions were
bound into a yoke; by his hand they were fastened together' (i. 12, 14). Five times over in this chapter, comes
the pathetic refrain 'there is none to comfort' her, for her
desolation is complete. And yet through all this lament
the one belief which survives the onslaught of their
troubles is that of the goodness of God and the justice of
His judgment. 'The Lord is in the right, for I have re-
belled against his word' (verse 18).

In the second chapter, this submissive attitude, in
which the sufferer accepts his punishment and retains
faith in the justice of God, is put under further strain, and
temporarily superseded by an overwhelming sense of
God's displeasure. 'The Lord has become like an enemy'
(verse 5) and in His anger He has destroyed them all.
They are beginning to reach the extremity of their
anguish. With the contempt of the neighbouring tribes
echoing in their ears on the one hand, and the cries of
their starving children coming to them on the other, they
begin to find refuge in prayer. 'Pour out your heart like
water before the presence of the Lord! Lift your hands to
him for the lives of your children, who faint for hunger
at the head of every street' (verse 19).

In this setting of the desperate plight of the nation, the
prophet proceeds to write of his own personal afflictions.
He believes that God is concerned with the pains of individuals, as well as of nations, and has a message of
judgment and redemption for the ones as well as for the
many. His is a sad story which enters the darkest night,
but it ends on a note in which he seems to trace Keats'
'budding morrow in midnight'. He first recounts how God
has dealt harshly with him. 'I am the man who has seen
affliction under the rod of his wrath; he has driven and
brought me into darkness without any light' (iii. 1, 2). At
times God has even seemed to put Himself out of reach of
prayer. 'Though I call and cry for help, he shuts out my

prayer' (verse 8). The sufferer is just on the point of suc-
cumbing to self-pity, when something makes him realize
there is no future in that, and he proceeds to cure himself in the best possible way, by recalling his blessings. In
spite of all the agonies he has just described, he has hope
(verse 21), a hope that centres in the mercy, compassion
and trustworthiness of God. 'The steadfast love of the
Lord never ceases, his mercies never come to an end; they
are new every morning; great is thy faithfulness. "The
Lord is my portion," says my soul, "therefore I will hope
in him." The Lord is good to those who wait for him, to
the soul that seeks him' (verses 22–25). He realizes how it
is only in the mercy of God that he is not suffering far
more than he is : for his sins deserve greater punishment.
He knows the meaning of God's compassion, a suffering
with him in his trouble that does not leave him to face it
alone. And he has now learnt to wait patiently for the deliverance that God will eventually bring him, for He is
faithful and will not let him down. This being so, he
argues, ought we ever to complain or question, when God,
who is sovereign over all, punishes us for our sins? (verses
37–39). No, rather we must search our hearts to see for
what sins He is calling us to repentance through the pains
brought upon us. 'Let us test and examine our ways, and
return to the Lord !' (verse 40). And where the issue is not
clear and the suffering cannot be surely traced to any
sins for which it may be punishment, then the writer turns
to God and commits himself and his problems to the
Judge who, whether we understand or not, will surely do
justly (verses 58, 59). Finally, in so far as his sufferings
were brought about by the cruelty and malice of his
enemies, God is called upon to act in judgment upon these
evil-doers, for did they not also deserve divine censure?
(verses 61–66).

The fourth chapter of this small book of Lamentations
is largely a poetic repetition of the sighing and sorrows of
God's people. Their land and dwellings, and even their
temple, are lying in ruins around them; the dead are
better off than the wounded or starving (verses 8, 9) and
cannibalism has broken out among them (verse 10);
young and old, rich and poor, are trying to scratch a

precarious livelihood from what had been left in the trail of their overthrow. In a final search for a scapegoat, the poet in bitterness turns upon the prophets and priests, and declares that their sins also have brought these troubles upon them (verses 13 ff.)—an accusation which is not answered. But his scorn is short-lived, and the Lamentations draw to a quieter end in prayer.

In this prayer we find no more railing against the wrath of God, but a humble call to look back and see how their sins had led to their present adversity, and then a final look upwards to see God on the throne, in control of even such violent forces as these, and a recognition that any affliction has value if it leads the sufferers back to God. 'Our fathers sinned, and are no more; and we bear their iniquities . . . The crown has fallen from our head; woe to us, for we have sinned!' (v. 7, 16). 'Thou, O Lord, dost reign for ever; thy throne endures to all generations . . . Restore us to thyself, O Lord, that we may be restored! Renew our days as of old! Or hast thou utterly rejected us? Art thou exceedingly angry with us?' (verses 19–22). The answer to this final query was the return of Israel from their seventy years' captivity, and the opportunity they were given of a new phase of national existence. God had not cast them off for ever, nor will He do so for any who turn to Him in their trouble, and repent them of their sins.

CHAPTER IV

AN ENEMY HAS DONE THIS

WE have seen that the Bible clearly portrays a state of affairs in which, on occasion, the sins of a man or a community have been followed by divine judgment in the form of some kind of suffering : it may be loss, disease or death. This was not invariably the case. When it did happen, when God dealt with a wrong-doer by way of immediate punishment, for instance, He sent a prophet or used some means of letting the wrong-doer know the meaning of his suffering, and giving him the opportunity to repent and mend his ways. Thus he came to learn a lesson through pain, which he could or would not learn in any other way. When no explanation was forthcoming, the sufferer could, it seems, assume at least that it was not due to his sins, though this suspicion, as we have seen, lingered long in the minds of the people.

What was true in this way of individuals, was also true of community life, for wrongdoing also often brought its painful penalty down upon the nation collectively. It is interesting, before we leave this subject, to note that the New Testament word for judgment is our English word 'crisis'. It bears out the Bible record of the fact that God does not order the affairs of the human race by slow evolutionary progress, but rather by many unpredictable interventions and crises, each of which has a measure of what we would call judgment. These might involve a natural calamity, the upheaval of a war, the incursion of some fiery prophet, or the supreme judgment of the crisis of the cross, of which we read, ' "Now is the judgment (crisis) of this world" . . . He said this to show by what death he was to die' (Jn. xii. 31–33). We readily acknowledge that the death of Christ on the cross was God's great act of salvation. It must be remembered that whenever God acted in judgment, it was not out of the vindictive spite of an irate father or an exasperated schoolmaster, but as a saving act. The God who 'sent the Son into the world, not to condemn the world, but that the world might be saved through him' (Jn. iii. 17), was the God of the Old Testament, no less than of the New. His ways certainly were not so well understood, nor was His nature so fully revealed, but as in the crisis of Christ's coming and death He was acting in judgment on the world in order to save it, so it is likely to have been in the pre-Christian era. P. T. Forsyth devotes a good deal of his book *The Justification of God* to developing this theme, and it is important that we should notice this, for if we can believe that God only punished in order to deliver, then the pain of the punishment becomes a worth-while thing. The bitterness that might arise against a God who punishes arbitrarily, could not survive in the assurance that it is simply His way of setting us free from our sin.

This brings us back to the difficult question of the connection between sin and suffering. If our sins sometimes bring suffering in their train as divine judgment (a judgment which is also a deliverance), then some connection must exist. We shall see, when we come to deal with the problem of sickness and divine healing, that many people naïvely equate the two, but it is not quite as simple as that. However, if we ask why God needs to use painful means of judgment, or why He needs to punish us ever at all, the answer must lie in the fact of sin. And it is because of this that God's judgments are saving judgments. He is 'forbearing toward you, not wishing that any should perish, but that all should reach repentance' (2 Pet. iii. 9).

Robert Burns, in his indignation against the inequalities of a society in which he himself held a privileged position while others had to search pathetically for employment, may appear to have a warped view of the world with his poem 'Man was made to mourn'. But this was not the morbid pessimism of a melancholic. It was righteous indignation against conditions arising long before the coming of the Welfare State, in which the sufferings of the unfortunate were part of the entail of public life. Indeed, as the Scriptures declare, 'Affliction does not come from the dust, nor does trouble sprout from the ground; but man is born to trouble as the sparks fly upward'—from the anvil of life on which his soul is battered into shape (Jb. v. 6, 7).

It is clear, then, that a great deal of human suffering can be directly attributed to the wrongdoing of man. If he were to repent and mend his ways, a vast surge of relief would go up from the human race, for so many of its pains would cease at the same time. We must accept the fact that we belong to a fallen race, a society in which the tendency to do wrong is predominant, and the consequences of giving way to this tendency are harmful to all. This liberty to sin will be discussed in the next chapter. The fact of it must be accepted now, and we must allow the Hebraic imagery of the serpent and the forbidden fruit, in the Genesis story of the fall, to illumine for us the truth that man has sinned and a storm of suffering has burst upon the world as a result. It is no fairy story or fanciful myth. Genesis chapter three gives poetic form to a truth without which the rest of the Bible does not make sense : that the origin of the miseries of this world lies not in God's original plan, but in the chaos brought about by man's sins. We read that part of the aftermath of man's disobedience is a spoiling of the perfection of nature as it left God's creative hand, particularly in relation to human life. Woman's natural function of childbirth, which in animals takes place without undue difficulty, becomes in our fallen humanity an act of pain, a shadow on the bliss of married life, a symbol of a fall from innocence (iii. 16). Man is condemned to toil with sweat of brow to extract his living from the natural resources of the earth, which, left untended, will run to seed and ruin (iii. 17–19) with thorns and thistles, the emblems of imperfection. Sin has left its mark, and men and women find even their most essential activities, of reproduction and the consumption of food, are not free from pain. Even the beauty of their physical form becomes a matter for shame and guilt (ii. 25, iii. 7, 10). All this is part of what Paul calls 'the mystery of iniquity' (2 Thes. ii. 7, AV), and what James, in his Epistle, describes as the breaking out into unsocial activity of the passions and corruptions that lie uncontrolled in human hearts (iv. 1, 2).

The Bible story speaks of a tempter who delighted in thus wrecking God's creation, and no understanding of the problem of evil which leaves out the personality of Satan can possibly be true. What Shakespeare called 'the slings and arrows of outrageous fortune', to the student of the Bible are the wounds of the arch enemy of God and good, who, for reasons we can hardly expect to fathom, has liberty of action in this present age, with endless possibilities of causing

> heart-ache and the thousand natural shocks
> That flesh is heir to . . .
> . . . the whips and scorns of time,
> Th' oppressor's wrong, the proud man's contumely,
> The pangs of despis'd love . . .

It may save us from experiencing such despair as Hamlet's if we can see that the New Testament teaches that much suffering, possibly all, is directly or indirectly of diabolical origin. The word 'Satan' means adversary. In the parable of the weeds which ruined the farmer's harvest, Jesus ex-

lained, 'An enemy has done this' (Mt. xiii. 28). The
adversary had been at work. In the case of the wretched
cripple woman who had been bent double by her complaint, Jesus said 'Satan has bound her' (see Lk. xiii. 16).
Paul, almost certainly writing of some personal physical
ailment which haunted him, called it 'a messenger of
Satan' (2 Cor. xii. 7). It is not in the least fanciful to
believe that among 'the works of the devil' (1 Jn. iii. 8)
which the Son of God came to destroy, human sickness
and suffering, as well as human sin, are included.

A large part of human suffering is undoubtedly inspired
by the devil. Pain is as natural an atmosphere in which
he can breathe as is sin. He finds his pleasure in stimu-
ating men to hurt one another, or to damage themselves,
and in many other ways the tale of human misery is a
running commentary on his diabolical activities. Suffering cannot be accounted for without reference to Satan,
and much Christian activity consists of direct conflict with
him in the field of affliction. The whole realm of medical
work and social service is a vast attempt to make good
the breaches in human well-being which have been made
by Satan. Jesus, Himself, spent as much time doing this as
He did in dealing with the more spiritual aspects of evil.
When He sent forth His disciples to deal with the sick
and suffering, He gave them 'authority . . . over all the
power of the enemy', and when they triumphed, He says
He Himself 'saw Satan fall like lightning from heaven'
Lk. x. 18, 19).

This is the more convincing when we look at the Old
Testament, particularly the book of Job where, in a
dramatic setting, we can read of a battle for the integrity
of a human soul between God and the devil. We are told,
first of all, that Job was a good man ('that man was
blameless and upright, one who feared God, and turned
away from evil', i. 1, 8, ii. 3), and therefore the spectators,
who are watching the drama unfold, know already what
is not disclosed to Job himself, that his sufferings at least
are not the punishment for his sins. When Satan confronts
God, he makes out that Job's integrity is false, and that
he fears God simply for what he can get out of it. Only
let some disaster overtake his crops and his flocks and
bring them down in ruin, and he will turn round and

curse God (i. 9–11). There then follows the tragic tale o
a sudden onslaught on Job's wealth and family and health
Armed raiders killed his employees and drove off hi
cattle; a thunderbolt destroyed his sheep and shepherds i
the field; his herd of camels was stolen; and finally
whirlwind demolished the house in which his sons wer
holding a party, and they were crushed to death (i. 13–19)
It was indeed a sorrowful story. Job had lost his fortun
and his family at one blow. But we find him rising t
remarkable heights of trust and triumph with word
which are repeated today whenever bereavement bring
mourners into the house of God : 'The Lord gave, and th
Lord has taken away; blessed be the name of the Lord

The second chapter of Job tells of a further attack upo
the unfortunate sufferer. It follows on Satan's argumen
that whereas a man like Job might possibly rise abov
such tragedy as he had already been through, as soon a
he began to feel pain in his own body, he would un
doubtedly give way. So we hear of him being struck dow
with a foul disease which broke out in 'loathsome sore
all over him. But yet again, and in spite of receiving n
help from his wife, who says, 'Better thou shouldst re
nounce God and have done with living' (ii. 9, Knox), Jo
sits in pain without a word of protest against his Make
'Shall we receive good at the hand of God, and shall w
not receive evil?' is his calm reply.

For the purposes of this present chapter, we will no
follow Job's story any further. The important thing t
notice here is the place given to the person of Satan i
Job's sufferings, which include not only physical illnes
but also, as we have seen, natural phenomena and th
warlike activities of his neighbours. The second causes
his troubles are traced back, in this profound book, to th
evil action of Satan, and this evil action to the permissio
of God Himself. 'The Lord said to Satan, "Behold, a
that he has is in your power; only upon himself do not pu
forth your hand" . . . "Behold, he is in your power; on
spare his life."' As far as Job himself was concerned, I
recognized even the loss of his all as having been th
direct activity of the Lord, who had 'taken away'. H
showed a true Hebrew insight into the overrulir
sovereignty of God in thus attributing his troubles, as we

as his joys, to the Lord. We, who study his story from the perspective of the biblical revelation, can see deeper. We understand that the prince of this world had been given limited opportunity to hurt, in order to test and demonstrate the invincible character of a soul who keeps near to God. The limit God placed on Satan's activity was, in the first instance, not to touch Job's physical health, and on the next occasion not to smite him with any fatal illness. Apart from this, no further rein curbed his powers of attack.

We see here, in dramatic form, the truth that Satan, for all his boasted independence, is in actual fact the servant of God. In spite of his limitations, Job himself recognized that God's hand showed itself in Satan's activity (ii. 10). Similarly Paul says of the 'messenger of Satan' that it was 'given' to him, we presume by God (2 Cor. xii. 7). Most of us find it hard to understand why God should permit the devil to appear all-powerful, and to bring such torture on human beings. Perhaps we could learn from Robinson Crusoe, who, when this problem weighed heavily on Man Friday's wakening intelligence, had an answer ready. ' "Well," says Friday, "you say God is so strong, so great; is He not much strong, much might as the devil?" "Yes, yes," says I, "Friday, God is stronger than the devil . . ." "But if God much strong, much might as the devil, why God no kill the devil, so make him no more do wicked?" "You may as well ask me," ' replies Crusoe after some anxious thought, ' "why does God not kill you and me when we do wicked things that offend Him." '

Before we leave this subject of the strange providence which allows God's world, and even the short span of a single human life, to be an arena in which divine and malignant forces rage a grim battle, we must remember that, great as the sufferer's pains so often are, God Himself is the greater sufferer. Theologians and pedants may argue about the impossibility of the 'passibility of the Godhead', but if God is like Jesus then we know He has a fellow-feeling with our pains. We have already seen some light on the problem of suffering, from the book of Lamentations in the Bible. There, also, we read that the writer had a firm faith in the power of God to share in the sufferings of His people. He writes, 'The steadfast love of the Lord never ceases, his mercies never come to an end . . . though he cause grief, he will have compassion according to the abundance of his steadfast love' (La. iii. 22, 32). In the Psalms, we find frequent references to almighty God as gracious and full of compassion (lxxxvi. 15, cxi. 4, cxlv. 8), especially longing to spare His people as much as possible of the suffering which comes to them as a result of their sins (lxxviii. 38). In Isaiah, the prophet, recounting 'the steadfast love of the Lord', says : 'He became their Saviour. In all their affliction he was afflicted' (lxiii. 8, 9).

When we turn to the New Testament, we read again and again how Jesus 'had compassion' on those He was hoping to help. This particular Greek word seems not to have been in classical use, but to have grown popular during the sufferings of the Jews in the pre-Christian era. It literally means 'being stirred to the depths'. The use of such a word to describe the feelings of our Lord when face to face with suffering people, must imply a far deeper degree of sympathy than normal. Indeed, in the compassion of Christ we see the true translation of love in relation to human trouble. His sympathy for the leper led Him to overcome the fears and prejudices of His time, and, 'moved with pity', actually to lay His hand upon the wretched, disfigured victim (Mk. i. 41). When He saw the crowds of men and women, as sick in soul as they were in body, it was 'moved with compassion' that Jesus urged His disciples to pray for more helpers to meet their needs (Mt. ix. 36 ff.). He felt the same when surrounded by the thousands who had denied themselves a midday meal to hear Him, and who looked like getting nothing to eat in the evening either, many of them being ill (Mt. xiv. 14). The sight of a widow burying her only son (Lk. vii. 13), and the groping of blind men as Jesus passed them in the throng (Mt. xx. 34), similarly moved His heart in loving compassion. In the two parables which best express the nature of God the Father, Jesus used the same word : the Good Samaritan having compassion on the wounded traveller, and the good father, compassion on the wayward son (Lk. x. 33, xv. 20).

The writer to the Hebrews tells us Jesus was 'touched with the feeling of our infirmities' (iv. 15, AV). Whenever

He came in contact with those who suffered, His heart went out to them in loving compassion and He brought help, healing and forgiveness. We believe that our Lord is still the same, and that the picture He gave in His own Person of the way God cares for His children when they are in trouble, is a true picture of the character and nature of our God still. That is the lesson Studdert Kennedy so graphically put into the mouth of his soldier in the trenches, a lesson we can learn to our infinite comfort : it matters to God about us (1 Pet. v. 7).

> How can it be that God can reign in glory,
>   Calmly content with what His love has done,
> Reading unmoved the piteous shameful story,
>   All the vile deeds men do beneath the sun?
>
> Are there no tears in the heart of the Eternal?
>   Is there no pain to pierce the soul of God?
> Then must He be a fiend of Hell infernal,
>   Beating the earth to pieces with His rod.
>
> Father, if He, the Christ, were Thy revealer,
>   Truly the first begotten of the Lord,
> Then must Thou be a suff'rer and a healer,
>   Pierced to the heart by the sorrow of the sword.
>
> Then must it mean, not only that Thy sorrow
>   Smote Thee that once upon the lonely tree,
> But that today, tonight and on the morrow
>   Still it will come, O gallant God, to Thee.

CHAPTER V

CAN SUFFERING EVER BE GOD'S WILL?

ONE of the most familiar remarks that a minister hears when he goes hospital visiting, or calling on some sick or tried person, is, 'I think this must be my cross.' This is said not only about painful accidents, or trying recurrent illnesses such as asthma or diabetes, but even about such experiences as having to live with an awkward mother-in-law or a fractious aunt. The idea in the back of the sufferer's mind is that God has selected a certain specific trouble and, for reasons which are seldom if ever made clear, has laid this upon the wretched person to bear. Almost any difficult circumstance could be spoken of in this way, and often is, but without a shred of evidence behind it. One has never met anyone who could say with confidence that God has made known to them that anything of this sort is their special cross. They always say, 'I suppose it must be.'

There is actually nothing in the Bible to suggest that God works in this way. As we have seen, there is an element of judgment in suffering, and we shall see later that divine chastening also often involves pain. But the cross is something very different. In the Christian sense, it is not an instrument of punishment or torture to those who *bear* it. Such a thought is quite foreign to our Lord's use of the term 'cross-bearing'. When He spoke about the cross His followers should carry (as distinct from His own crucifixion), He used the words 'take' (Mt. x. 38), 'bear' (Lk. xiv. 27), or 'take up' (Mt. xvi. 24; Mk. viii. 34; Lk. ix. 23). A study of these passages (the only ones in which the phrase occurs) suggests two things. Firstly, that the cross He was speaking about was something to be voluntarily undertaken, and secondly that it is an essential part of our Christian discipleship. There is nothing arbitrary about bearing a cross. God does not lay it on one and not on another. *Every* true Christian should be bearing his cross every day, and doing so by choice and gladly as a sign of his devotion to his Lord.

This is not the place to discuss what Christian discipleship entails.[1] It will be sufficient to notice that the context of these sayings of Jesus, already quoted, shows that they refer primarily to discipline and sacrifice, not to suffering or distress. To be a Christian is to put devotion to Christ before even family loyalty; to value spiritual riches more than worldly wealth; to follow the will of God and not one's own inclinations. A man was expected to count the cost of this before embarking on the Christian life (Lk. xiv. 28-33), which implies his liberty either to refuse the cross, if he so wished, or to take it up as a daily discipline, which, while it might certainly bring suffering on the grounds of

[1] See the author's *Henceforth*, p. 19.

his Christian convictions (see Chapter 9), has no direct connection with suffering in general. It is time that Christians taught more clearly this meaning of the cross, so that it need no longer be confused with the apparently haphazard coming of pain or affliction or trouble.

We get a similar confusion of thought when we consider whether or not God wills us to suffer. If someone is not sighing about his trouble being 'a cross', one is likely to hear, through the moans or tears of the sufferer, the phrase : 'I suppose this must be the will of God.' So commonly is trouble labelled 'the will of God' that the popular idea of God seems to be someone who takes pleasure in making His creatures miserable. Is it not strange that it is almost always in the context of pain that we hear people talk about 'the will of God', as if God never willed us anything pleasant at all? Before we try to answer the question 'Is suffering ever God's will?' we ought to remind ourselves that, primarily, the will of God is something wonderful; something to be sought and enjoyed; something to be engaged in; a positive and inspiring activity.

The Psalmist, as he reflected on the wonderful ways of God in his life, lifting him out of the mire and putting a new song in his mouth, cried out in joy, 'I delight to do thy will, O my God' (xl. 8). When Paul wrote to the church at Rome, urging them to surrender all their powers of mind and body to the service of God, he described the will of God as 'good and acceptable and perfect' (xii. 2). Here was nothing to be groaned about or regretted, but something to be put to the test in their daily lives, and 'proved' to be altogether more wonderful than anything they were likely to discover if they remained conformed to the pattern of worldly life.

In the Lord's Prayer, the will of God is closely associated with the idea of the kingdom of God : 'Thy kingdom come, thy will be done.' To a Christian, the kingdom of God is the sphere of his every action. It is his one hope of the future, and his chief interest in the present. The extension of the kingdom of God he believes to be a most important part of the will of God, and he takes a delighted share in it, with this in mind. So, to the Christian, the will of God is something to be 'done' rather than 'suffered'. It is a great and positive spiritual activity, which dominates his whole life and demands all his powers. It calls for consecration and devotion, and when he is surrendered to it, gives him a wholly absorbing and thrilling sphere of service : the extension of the kingdom of God. The will of God, then, is primarily something to be looked for and then gladly welcomed. It is time we omitted from our church services those hymns (and sermons) which imply that *invariably* 'across the will of nature leads on the path of God'.

But of course there undoubtedly are times when the will of God does run counter to our natural inclinations, especially when God expects us to ascend Hill Difficulty, and, like the famous Pilgrim's two companions, we seek an easy way round instead. Jesus, Himself, was frequently tempted to do the same. At the outset of His career, the devil urged Him in the wilderness to gain the kingdoms of the world for which He was going to die, without having to suffer the pains of death. But Jesus chose God's way. After the wild enthusiasm of His entry into Jerusalem had turned into the grim opposition which sent Jesus to the cross, He was again sorely tempted to find a less painful way of fulfilling His Father's will. 'Now is my soul troubled', He cried. 'And what shall I say, "Father, save me from this hour"? No, for this purpose I have come to this hour. Father, glorify thy name' (Jn. xii. 27, 28). As the crowds thought it was thundering, Jesus heard the divine voice which confirmed His destiny. He then told them that His mind was made up, and His death by violence was unavoidable. Again, in the garden of Gethsemane, Jesus was once more hard put to it not to seek an easier path. But after the most intense spiritual struggle, which itself appears to have been fraught with physical pain and extreme mental torture, He won the conflict and pledged His will to that of the Father. 'Not my will, but thine, be done.' There was, of course, more than mere resignation in these words of our Lord's. He realized, as He had hinted in the prayer He taught the disciples on the mount, that God's will is not something to be endured but something to be accomplished. So into the hands of wicked men He freely committed Himself, and 'the pains which he endured our salvation have procured'.

When Jesus thus went to the cross, it was to fight the evil which was to nail Him there. He accepted the painful hostility of Jerusalem, because it was a necessary part of His great redeeming work. He fought to the last ounce of His strength the powers of darkness whose activity has overshadowed human history since man's fall from innocence, and His body, and even His heart, were broken in the process. From this we learn that the will of God may well involve us, also, in a struggle, and many good people's sufferings can surely be regarded as wounds inflicted in battle. Miss Amy Carmichael, who devoted all her life to attacking the evils of child prostitution in Hindu temples, used to hate being referred to, when her activities had led to illness of any kind, as being *hors de combat*. She used to feel quite offended at the suggestion that she was 'laid aside' by sickness, like a cracked china cup put out of harm's reach on the shelf. For her, as for all Christians with the warrior spirit, any time of sickness was simply like being treated for wounds in order to be fit enough to go back to the fight. Much of the suffering we endure is surely permitted in order to be attacked and overcome, and in this process of resistance, we become the stronger for future fray. We must beware, then, too easy an acquiescence in suffering as the will of God, lest it make us feeble, whereas it should be making us strong.

There are a number of Christian people who, while they would not deny that there is a place in the plan of almighty God for misfortunes of some kind, yet claim that sickness and pain in particular can never be in the will of God.[1] They do not claim that man can be spared the ordinary miseries of life in a sinful world, but they do seem convinced that he should never be ill. The inconsistency of this is lost under the sense that sickness of the body is a supreme evil. They are sure that God loves us

---

[1] e.g. 'It is hard to understand how converted Christian people can accept sickness as part of God's will for them.'
  (F. L. Wyman, *Healing through Christ*, p. 23.)
'Disease never comes from God, is always contrary to God's will, and God always desires to heal.'
  (Richard Spread, *Stretching Forth Thy Hand to Heal*, p. 33.)
'I believe implicitly that God means us all to be free—free from sin, pain, accidents and mental and physical conflict.'
  (Christopher Woodard, *A Doctor's Faith is Challenged*, p. 43.)

so much that He could never wish us to be sick. Such people are in grave danger, it would seem, of saying that God always wants life to be comfortable for us; that we do not require the discipline of hardship; that we are to be spared any kind of rod, and yet not be spoiled children. Is this the God of the Bible, or some sentimental picture conjured up in the imagination of particularly sensitive writers? Does God really want His children to be preserved from *all* pain? If so, was Peter wrong when he referred to his readers 'suffering according to God's will'? (See 1 Pet. iv. 19, etc.)

Believing that sickness and the love of God are incompatible leaves more questions unanswered than answered, such as Paul's thorn in the flesh, and the diseases of godly people who have radiantly accepted them as part of God's purpose. On the other hand, it is equally false to argue that suffering is *always* the will of God, that it is necessarily some kind of punishment on our misdeeds, or even that it is 'sent' by a sovereign God, in every case, for our good. If there is something in the consciousness of us all which revolts against the suggestions that suffering is never God's will or always God's will, we must search for a synthesis, if one is to be found. And if it can satisfy the enlightened theologians as well as the benighted sufferer, so much the better. If it is true, it should do so. But truth is so much greater than our apprehension of it, that we have to face the probability that in considering such a mystery as the purposes of almighty God, it is possible we shall sometimes be mistaken, and it is likely we shall often be bewildered.

If we are right in accepting the view that suffering, like sin, is part of the inheritance of our fallen race, and that sickness and misery are often, like sin, too, signs in the field of happiness that 'an enemy has done this', then we are faced with the task of finding a *via media* between laying the blame upon God, the devil, or on man himself. We refuse to lay it on God. To say it is the fault of man himself only accounts for a proportion of his pains. To blame Satan, which, as we have seen, the Scriptures often show to be true, only raises the further question of why God allows this. We must find where these lines of thought converge, the place where my faith and my reason can find satisfaction. In looking for this point we realize that we are like junior draughtsmen in an architect's office, faintly and probably faultily guessing at the over-all plan, yet seeing just enough to feel we can at least appreciate its complicated nature.

We have suggested so far that it cannot fairly be said of *every* particular calamity, 'This is the will of God', in the sense that God brought it about for some inscrutable reason of His own. We have also assumed, as believers in a God of love, that we are not the pawns of an impersonal Fate such as Omar Khayyám described when he sang—

'Tis all a Chequer-board of Nights and Days
Where Destiny with Men for Pieces plays;
   Hither and thither moves, and mates, and slays,
And one by one back in the Closet lays.

Nor do we believe that life is entirely haphazard, and we who suffer are doing so in much the same way as snowflakes are blown into the muck of a gutter by the unpredictable vagaries of the wind. We cling to the belief with which we started our thinking at the beginning, that God is a Father who loves His creatures and wishes them well. But by this word 'well' we mean not necessarily a full physical freedom from disease or illness. We mean health of heart : true godliness and goodness, which shows itself normally in health of mind and body, but also accepts the opposite, for what it can do for us. God knows what the best is, and knows best how to bring it about for us.

This brings us to the second great belief to which we gave some thought earlier on, the fact of the sovereignty of God. Christian faith is faith in a God who has oversight and control over the affairs of the whole world. He is the God of Nature who answered Job out of the whirlwind, and taught him the lesson we need to learn at this point. All the forces of creation are under God's hand, and the aspects man can see of Nature's glory 'are but the outskirts of his ways' (Jb. xxvi. 14). If this is so, then how can man expect fully to understand the ways of providence, or trace the will of God in the complicated circumstances of life? 'Where were you', asks the Almighty, 'when I laid the foundation of the earth? Tell me, if you have understanding.' In magnificent imagery Job is made to sense the wonder of God's power, and the impertinence of trying to fathom the ways of providence. 'Then Job answered the Lord : "Behold, I am of small account; what shall I answer thee? I lay my hand on my mouth. I have spoken once, and I will not answer; twice, but I will proceed no further"' (xxxviii. 4, xl. 3–5). We would do well to follow his example, rather than try to parcel and ticket the mysterious happenings of life as if we clearly understood them all. Job, of course, knew less about the meaning of his sufferings than we do, for in this story the veil has been withdrawn to show us Satan in the presence of God. In considering the will of God we must acknowledge that, on the basis of that evidence, together with many other references elsewhere in the Bible, the activities of Satan are within the orbit of divine oversight. He parades as 'prince of this world' in temporary liberty, but belief in the overruling power of God prevents us thinking that Satan's freedom to harm God's world is without limitations or end.

Let us sum up where our thoughts have so far brought us. The will of God, He being what and who He is, must be good and perfect and acceptable, to be sought after, and welcomed when discovered. It will involve on our part not just passive submission, but active co-operation. In the course of following this will of God, it is almost certain that opposition from Satan will show itself, probably in some form of suffering or trouble. But this cannot frustrate the ultimate purposes of God. It might, however, involve an apparent temporary set-back. The healing ministry and health-giving teaching of Christ show that God does not normally wish His creatures to suffer, any more than that they should sin, and the battle against suffering, as that against moral evil, is a battle led by the Lord. But this is only idealistically true. It describes God's perfect will, but does not account for God's adaptation of this perfect will to the conditions of a fallen race. Much confusion can arise if we do not recognize that the ideal of complete freedom from either sin or suffering is unattainable in the circumstances of human life. This does not mean that conflict against them is a waste of energy. By no means can one say that, with the biblical record of redemption before us. But we must accept the facts of our sad condition, the fruit of the misuse of man's freewill. I may be difficult for us to explain to the sceptical mind why we think God allowed man to misuse his freedom, or Satan to wreak such damage on the earth. But the alternative belief, that God should force man into doing His will and prevent him from doing evil, demands even greater justification, for it would leave mankind no longer a race of responsible men and women. In any case, we are basing our thinking on the record in the Bible, which, as we have seen, shows Satan in the shadows, with liberty to bring pain and to encourage others to do the same—the Lord God Almighty always retaining the power to say to evil what He could say to the tide, 'Thus far shall you come, and no farther, and here shall your proud waves be stayed' (Jb. xxxviii. 11).

This all means that in the working out of God's purposes for man, due allowance has to be made for the wilfulness and sin which delay the steady progress of His will. A bypass is often made in God's providential guidance of His children, when their advance along the line of His primary plan is halted. We see it in the history of His dealings with the children of Israel of old. God had made known to them His will that they should be delivered from the slave conditions of life in Egypt, into the national independence which the promised land offered them. But because they proved themselves unfit for these new responsibilities, they had to make a wide and lengthy detour for forty years in the desert. During this time, their sufferings brought home to them lessons they would learn in no other way, and without which they would not be ready to do God's will. In that event, there appeared to be what we might call a secondary, permissive, and very flexible will of God which restrained those who travelled along it from wandering too far, and brought them back, eventually, to the path their sin made them unfit to travel at first. We see the same principle at work in the story of the prodigal son, who failed to rise to the responsibility of independence by spending his fortune as his father would have wished. His return home, as a wiser and humbler man, meant that the father could do much more for him then than before his visit to the far country. The temporary delay was unfortunate but inevitable. The father's will was bypassed for a while, but finally fulfilled. In this kind of way we can believe that God continually works out His sovereign purpose in His own time, with the divine wisdom which adapts itself to the persons and circumstances involved.

A beautiful illustration of this has been described by Miss Amy Carmichael [1] and Dr. Leslie Weatherhead. [2] In the days when carpets were made by hand in Persia, the weaving was done on a vertical framework, with the designer on one side and the weavers on the other. The artist called out the colours to the workers as he wished, for he could see what was hidden from them, the slow evolution of the design in his mind. The plan thus gradually took shape, and even if one of the weavers made a mistake and inserted the wrong coloured thread, the artistic skill of the designer was such that *he could alter his first plan and adapt it to include the mistake.* No human frailty or sin can utterly mar the handiwork of the great Designer whose wise guidance of the affairs of His children has a certain divine flexibility about it. And we, who try to trace some part of our troubles as being incorporated in the will of God, will not say with confidence that this which I am undergoing just now 'is the will of God', but rather : 'It is certainly *within* the will of God.' We can see God drawing into the pattern of His purposes all the many stray threads in our lives, in a way which seems so meaningless to the man of no faith, so mysterious to the man of a little, and so wonderful to the humble and repentant believer.

From the point of view of the subject of this book, the important thing to notice is that whenever the ideal will of God is frustrated, and His permissive plans begin to operate, it is as certain that a degree of pain and suffering are involved as it is that sin and evil make the detour necessary. In such situations we are bound to ask, in the great over-all picture of God ruling the world He loves, What happens about these things? Does He treat sin and suffering in the same way? Is He equally against them both? That great theologian of a former generation, P. T. Forsyth, has written about this important question : 'All sin is an ill, but an ill is not a sin, nor is it caused by it. Suffering abounded in the animal world before man

[1] *Rose from Brier*, p. 159.   [2] *Why do Men Suffer?*, p. 150.

appeared with the moral freedom that makes sin possible. Pain came before sin, and, as it has no connection with freedom, it is non-moral. And in any theodicy, or justification of God, His treatment of the two is different, to our Christian faith at least. The power in Him can convert suffering to a sacrament, but it must destroy sin. It can transcend and sanctify suffering while the suffering remains, but sin it must abolish. The cross of Christ can submerge suffering, and make it a means of salvation, but with sin it can make neither use nor terms; it can only make an end of it. God in Christ is capable of suffering and of transmuting sorrow; but of sin He is incapable, and His work is to destroy it.' [1] If he is right, then it is not true that God always and in all circumstances wishes to abolish pain. If He can make suffering a sacrament, and if He allowed His Son to suffer as He did, then are we ever right to pray that we may be set free from our ills?

This brings us to raise the question, Can prayer change God's will, or does it only change us? First of all let us freely admit, as we shall see later in this book, that we are frequently in no right mood to face suffering. If we pray for deliverance without being willing to do God's will, we can hardly expect our prayers to be answered. The pattern prayer of Gethsemane, 'Not my will, but thine, be done', will condemn us. One of the results of prayer is to change the pray-er. As we seek God's face, which in the case of distress we do often in desperation and real earnest, we are likely to be driven to cry out in the end, 'Oh God, Thou knowest best, Thou knowest our needs, our hopes, our deep trouble.' From there it is not a long way to praying: 'Do the best for us, O God; let us know what Thy will is, and make us willing to accept it.'

There are good Christians who argue that such a prayer as this displays too easy an acceptance of trouble as inevitably the will of God. In the Gospel of Luke, they remind us, Jesus told men 'always to pray and not lose heart' (xviii. 1). He illustrated this with the story of the judge who was bothered by a widow whose cause he did not want to sponsor, but who eventually gave in to her persistent praying. P. T. Forsyth has an important passage in which he warns us against too easy a resignation to

[1] *The Justification of God*, pp. 138 ff.

what we think may be the will of God. 'We say too soon, "Thy will be done"; and too ready acceptance of a situation as his will often means feebleness or sloth. It may be his will that we surmount his will. It may be his higher will that we resist his lower. Prayer is an act of the will much more than of sentiment, and its triumph is more than acquiescence.[1] We would do well to learn this lesson, for there are many cases of illness and trouble in which persistent prayer has worked wonders. This is not to suggest that in every case we are intended to pray without ceasing with a specific answer in mind. Many believers in divine healing tell us we should do this in faith that recovery will come if we persist enough. The number of cases in which this does not happen reminds us that it cannot necessarily be so. But there are times when it is certainly right to persist in wrestling with God, just as there are other times when it is equally as much an act of faith to lay the matter before God and accept the answer as His revealed will. In these different situations one must believe that God shows us, if we ask Him, whether we are to pray through till we see the anticipated answer, or whether to accept the suffering concerned in a willing and submissive spirit.

An illustration of this comes in that remarkable book *Margaret*.[2] She was a girl of fifteen who came into a wonderful faith in Christ while her life was gradually drawing to an end through the ravages of cancer. The turning-point in her life, and in the lives of those who loved her, came quite definitely when their persistent prayers for her recovery gave way to a quiet acceptance that, in her case, God's will was that she should not recover. The number of people who have been led to faith in Christ through this wonderful story leads one to believe that we are by no means always expected to go on praying for the recovery of the sick or troubled in every case.

However, we must keep the balance in this matter, and with the weighty authority of so great a theologian as Forsyth behind us we must anxiously consider his contention that : 'Prayer may really change the will of God, or if not his will, his intention.'[3] As we begin to pray we become more conformable to the will of God, who then

[1] *The Soul of Prayer*, p. 124. [2] p. 60. [3] *op. cit.*, p. 124.

begins to act differently with us from the way in which He began. We change, if not the will, the conduct of God towards us. As we go on praying we become more spiritually ready for the answer, and instead of God giving us our request at once and sending leanness into our soul (Ps. cvi. 15), we gain by the delay which causes Him to treat with us in a different way from that in which He began. Prayer, then, is the way in which we can co-operate with the flexibility of God's will as it embraces all ills and turns them to our ultimate good.

In an age which provided its dark background of the sufferings of the slaves in North America, that great Quaker poet, Whittier, wrote of a following of the will of God which did not merely accept evil as inevitable, nor sought an easy way out. He saw their struggles as part of the battle with God against evil, encouraged by the hope that a future generation might benefit from the pains of the present one. For them the will of God was something which it was a glory to try to find and then to carry out, and the faith that shines out from them can illumine our path also :—

> We see not, know not; all our way
> Is night—with Thee alone is day;
> From out the torrent's troubled drift,
> Above the storm our prayers we lift,
>   Thy will be done!
>
> The flesh may fade, the heart may faint,
> But who are we to make complaint,
> Or dare to plead, in times like these,
> The weakness of our love of ease?
>   Thy will be done!
>
> We take with solemn thankfulness
> Our burden up, nor ask it less,
> And count it joy that even we
> May suffer, serve, or wait for Thee,
>   Whose will be done!
>
> Though dim as yet in tint and line,
> We trace Thy picture's wise design,
> And thank Thee that our age supplies
> Its dark relief of sacrifice,
>   Thy will be done!

> If for the age to come, this hour
> Of trial hath vicarious power,
> And, blest by Thee, our present pain,
> Be liberty's eternal gain,
> Thy will be done!

CHAPTER VI

SPIRITUAL HEALING

WE have touched on the fact that many devout Christians sincerely believe that God always wills our health, and therefore that we can and should claim His healing for every kind of sickness at all times. This is an aspect of the problem of suffering which deserves further examination, for there is wide divergence of opinion in the matter. Many equally earnest Christians do not accept the suggestion that God invariably wishes to heal and that it is therefore sin or lack of faith that prevents Him from doing so.

We can start our thinking from the belief that *normally* God, being the God of beauty and goodness, wills the full health of the body, mind and spirit of the children whom He has created. The Bible shows that sickness as well as sin is an object of God's redemptive work. Israel's great evangelistic prophet saw this vision when he wrote, 'He was wounded for our transgressions . . . and with his stripes we are healed' (Is. liii. 5). The Psalmist includes good health as a blessing for which to thank God: 'Bless the Lord, O my soul, and forget not all his benefits, who forgives all your iniquity, who heals all your diseases' (Ps. ciii. 2, 3). Matthew records that the exorcism of evil spirits and acts of healing were often inseparable. 'He cast out the spirits with a word, and healed all who were sick. This was to fulfil what was spoken by the prophet Isaiah, "He took our infirmities and bore our diseases"' (Mt. viii. 16, 17). Peter repeats Isaiah's prophecy: 'He himself bore our sins in his body on the tree . . . By his wounds you have been healed' (1 Pet. ii. 24).

Indeed, it is not easy to separate the healing of the body from that of the soul—for the soul (or spirit if one likes) sins through the body, and a sick body often conceals a sick soul. Jesus said to the paralysed man, after He had healed him, 'See, you are well! Sin no more, that nothing worse befall you' (Jn. v. 14). His first words to a similarly stricken man were: 'Take heart, my son; your sins are forgiven' (Mt. ix. 2). The apostle James made it a condition of healing in answer to the prayers of the Christian brotherhood, that the sufferer should first confess his sins (v. 16). Dr. André Schlemmer points out that many sicknesses arise from a sinful desire for excess of pleasure, or from lack of self-control. 'The glutton who continually eats unwisely, the lazy person who allows himself to grow fat, the ambitious or excitable man who over-works, the man of moods who obeys no rules—all these by their own indulgence continually violate the laws of human life.'[1]

Salvation and redemption, sanctification and holiness are great spheres of divine activity on behalf of God's children which, under the general title of healing, involve the whole personality. The Bible concept of God suggests that He does not normally wish our sins to be forgiven but our bodies to continue maimed. Christ's work was, and many believe still is, operative in both spheres. We need to remember that the body with which God has endowed us is a gift we receive from His hand, and we are responsible for keeping it in health and fitness. Much of the book Leviticus is devoted to impressing on the children of Israel the divine authority behind simple rules of hygiene. When we come to the fact of the incarnation, we find God honouring the human body as the vehicle for His own indwelling in the Person of Christ. To what He so deigned to use in this way we must give all possible respect. Moreover, as Dr. Weatherhead points out, 'God created the body to be the perfect instrument of the spirit. It cannot be his will that it should function imperfectly, or that man should assent to disease without doing everything possible to attain health. God's primary will is perfect health.'[2] Most Christians would agree with him here. Because of this, Paul urged his readers many times to

[1] *Faith and Medicine*, p. 27.
[2] *Psychology, Religion and Healing*, p. 401.

avoid especially those sins which defile or destroy the body, which is the temple of the Holy Spirit (1 Cor. iii. 16). 'The body is not meant for immorality, but for the Lord' (1 Cor. vi. 13–20). We are to 'glorify God' in our bodies and present them to God as living sacrifices, the means whereby we can go into the world to carry out God's perfect will (Rom. xii. 1, 2).

We must therefore accept the contention that God normally desires full health and freedom from pain for mankind, on a number of grounds. Firstly, because only so do we approximate to the perfection of our creation; secondly, because our Lord sanctified the body by His use of it; thirdly, because God mystically, but none the less really, dwells within the body of individual believers by His Spirit, as He does in the body of Christ, the Church itself; fourthly, because much sickness, as we have seen, is linked with sin and is the work of Satan, and therefore cannot be accepted without protest or conflict. Finally, we believe God is on the side of health because of the frequent references to this which we find in so many parts of the Bible. We read, for instance, of the children of Israel as they began their wanderings after release from Egypt, that God promised that if they followed the way of life which He planned for them, He would care for their health in the hazardous experiences of desert travel which lay before them. 'If you will diligently hearken to the voice of the Lord your God . . . I will put none of the diseases upon you which I put upon the Egyptians; for I am the Lord, your healer . . . You shall serve the Lord your God, and I will bless your bread and your water; and I will take sickness away from the midst of you' (Ex. xv. 26, xxiii. 25).

The prophet Jeremiah, in recalling his people to a consciousness of their sinfulness, promises them not only God's forgiveness but also full healing for the scars of their sufferings in captivity. 'I will restore health to you, and your wounds I will heal, says the Lord' (Je. xxx. 17). Malachi also has a vision of the healing power of the Lord in his magnificent message in which God says : 'For you who fear my name the sun of righteousness shall rise, with healing in its wings' (iv. 2). When Jesus launched His twelve disciples on their first evangelistic tour, their marching orders included both the preaching of the gospel and the ministry of healing. 'He called the twelve together and gave them power and authority over all demons and to cure diseases, and he sent them out to preach the kingdom of God and to heal' (Lk. ix. 1, 2). When, later, He sent out seventy of them two by two, they received the same injunction. 'Whenever you enter a town and they receive you . . . heal the sick in it and say to them, "The kingdom of God has come near to you"' (Lk. x. 8, 9).

The establishment and extension ('coming') of the kingdom of God is, as we have already seen, the dominant feature of the will of God. The work of healing diseases is a vitally important activity in the kingdom of God. It is fair, therefore, to assume that any healing ministry, be it that of the medical profession or the consecrated lay healer, must normally be working along the line of the will of God. This belief is strengthened when we remember that our Lord's last commission to His disciples was to include such a ministry : 'He said unto them, Go ye into all the world, and preach the gospel to every creature . . . these signs shall follow them that believe . . . they shall lay hands on the sick, and they shall recover' (Mk. xvi. 15, 17, 18, AV). When we come to read the story of the early Church in action in the book of the Acts, the same emphasis is found. The apostles frequently exert a healing ministry (iii. 7, 8, v. 15, 16, ix. 32–35, xiv. 8–10, xix. 12, xxviii. 8).

If we add to all this the enormous place that healing took in the life of our Lord Himself, the evidence is overwhelming. Amongst those whose sufferings Jesus relieved by restoration to sound health, were lepers and cripples, the blind, deaf and dumb, victims of paralysis, epilepsy and insanity, and multitudes of others. Any of us who claim to follow Him must feel that this work of His should go on still in these post-New Testament times, and that Christ's Church should be in the forefront of all such activity, for two main reasons. Firstly, because of the great compassion of Jesus, which we believe to be still part of His glorified nature. This Christian humanitarian spirit is a legacy we have inherited from Him, and has been the inspiration of most social service in the world since. Jesus told us that love in action is to be our duty to our neighbour, and for that reason alone we should exert all our energies in the relief of pain and suffering, as Jesus did. Secondly, we are called to this by virtue of our believing it to be the will of God. Our duty to God demands it of us. If we love Him we will engage, on His behalf, in the conflict of good against evil, of health against sickness. We shall do this all the more readily as we learn from the supreme Psychologist, Jesus, who 'knew what was in man'. By the way in which He administered His healing touches He showed the link between the sins and sufferings of those who came to Him. This is not our subject here, but a fascinating study awaits those who will follow this aspect of our Lord's great insight into the root causes of men's miseries, and how He dealt with them there in the depths of their being.

In the light of all we have seen, there are many who argue that the Christian Church should still be exercising a healing ministry of the same degree today, and only fails to do so through apathy, ignorance or spiritual decline. In most branches of the Christian Church the healing side of the ministry is receiving more attention now than for many years. Others, many Christian doctors amongst them, sincerely believe that the gift of miraculous healing was withdrawn from the Church after the New Testament era and that it is wrong to look for any repetition of New Testament miracles today. They base their case on two points. The first, which would hardly be disputed by anyone, is that the science of preventive and therapeutic medicine and surgery are gifts of God in themselves, and that those who employ them in the battle against injury, disease and malnutrition are doing God's healing work today with the added skills and knowledge with which twentieth-century science has endowed them. These Christian medical men would not deny that unusual phenomena do occasionally occur, though they are very sceptical of the cures claimed by lay healers. They feel for the most part that God heals in this present era through normal medical channels, and that other healers are either in danger of raising false hopes, or of dealing superficially with troubles which they do not always understand. Their second reason for being suspicious of healing which is practised outside the medical profession, is that modern science has recently made so many discoveries in the realms of psycho-somatic disease that experts in psychiatry and psychotherapy are needed to deal with a vast number of the illnesses which fill our hospitals today. Mental curative treatment they feel should not be left to amateurs, though they would be the first to agree that faith and the will to recover are of prime importance.

Those who are ardent believers in miraculous healing must be tolerant in their attitude to those who disagree with them. The medical profession has done untold good in the relief of suffering throughout the world to a degree which no non-professional healers could possibly hope to reach. Christian doctors and surgeons, on the other hand, must beware of professional jealousy blinding them to the limitations of their own powers of diagnosis and treatment, and to the possibility of supra-natural visitations by the God whom the Bible tells us is the Healer, and whose ways can neither be foretold nor neatly pigeon-holed afterwards. There is an element of inscrutability in the New Testament about the powers of healing which Christ bestowed on His Church. In the first instance this authority was limited to the twelve apostles (Lk. ix. 1, 2, 6), and then to the seventy (Lk. x. 1–9). The writer to the Hebrews (ii. 4) suggests that God disposed of His miracle-working power 'according to his own will', and not indiscriminately on all believers. Paul, writing to the Corinthians (1 Cor. xii. 28–30), asked the question, 'Do all work miracles? Do all possess gifts of healing?' which assumed the existence of these capabilities but did not expect every Christian to have them. He states that 'the same Spirit' who gave wisdom, knowledge and faith, also bestowed the gift of healing 'dividing to every man severally as he will' (1 Cor. xii. 11, AV). Paul's own gift of healing does not always seem to have been used, for he was unable to heal himself, or Timothy (1 Tim. v. 23), and he left Trophimus sick at Miletus (2 Tim. iv. 20). From this we deduce that while all Christians should, in their prayers and service, be actively engaged in the general battle against sickness, the actual gift of a power to work seeming miracles by the grace of God is by no means given to all; nor is it given to any all the time. Indeed, there are even suggestions that some healing may be accomplished by evil powers, working as angels of light. Jesus Himself acknowledged that the magicians of His day had the power to invoke the arch-demon Beelzebul and cast out evil spirits in that way (Lk. xi. 19).

It would seem that God entrusted the great responsibility of working healing to those like Peter and John (Acts iii. 1-8), and Paul (Acts xiv. 8-10, xx. 9-12), whom He had tested and found worthy. Not everyone is fitted for such a calling, for it often involves a struggle with the powers of evil themselves (see Mk. ix. 25, 26; Lk. iv. 35), and demands great consecration of spirit and much expenditure of spiritual force. When Jesus cured the woman who had suffered so long from unnatural haemorrhage, He said 'I perceive that power has gone forth from me' (Lk. viii. 46). This seems to have happened whenever He healed the sick (Lk. vi. 19) and must have added greatly to the strain of His self-giving in this way. Similar physical demands are made on all who give themselves to this kind of ministry.

It is not really within the purpose of this book to argue the point whether all Christian people, or some, or none, should exercise the gift or become the channel of divine healing. It is, however, worth pointing out how much personal suffering could be alleviated if we understood better the close links that exist between the mind and the body, and the manner in which our faith can be a firm ally to the processes of healing which medical science or the ministry of the clergy might use. More people are sick today because they are unhappy, than unhappy because they are sick. The close association between mental states and physical reactions shown, for instance, in the sinking feeling in the pit of the stomach of a schoolboy outside the headmaster's study, or in changes in the colour of the complexion in conditions of embarrassment, anger or fear, bears this out. The use of the lie-detector is based on the alterations of heartbeat and blood pressure

SPIRITUAL HEALING 73

due to the disturbance of the thoughts and even of the conscience. Moreover, gastric ulcers, some skin complaints, temporary paralysis, and even arthritis and asthma are now acknowledged to be often connected with mental dis-ease and stress. Also, there is the great discovery of psychology which teaches us that the unconscious mind lies, like the bulk of an iceberg, below the surface of the apparent mind, and contains within it, in the form of repressed suggestions and conflicts, vast potentiality of disturbance.

In addition to all this, doctors will agree that depression, despair, pessimism and fear are certain to delay healing. This is why many members of the medical profession try, not always successfully, and in the writer's opinion very questionably,to conceal from the patient the seriousness of his condition. On the other hand, 'A cheerful heart is a good medicine, but a downcast spirit dries up the bones' (Pr. xvii. 22). Hope, courage, buoyancy of spirit, and cheerfulness will speed the processes of healing, and much of the calling of the nursing profession is engaged in this work which they do so wonderfully. If the sufferer has convinced faith in Christ, the likelihood of his recovery is so much the more. Many people would say it was certain. They think that the reason why so many do not recover and why so many prayers seem to go unanswered is because of lack of faith on the part of the patient or his friends. They find strong support for this view in the passage (Mt. xiii. 58) where we read : 'He did not do many mighty works there, because of their unbelief.' There is no doubt that normally Christ demanded faith in those He was about to cure. On the other hand, it is clear from such a passage as Hebrews xi (especially verses 36–39) that faith is no sure means of escape or of recovery, only of the power to endure. It cannot be established that Jesus always healed every sick person He came across, or that His disciples did the same. The humble Christian is content to leave this mysterious question to be answered, along with so many others, in the hereafter.

Nothing can be assuredly argued from this except that the place of faith in healing is not as simple as some make out. It is certainly no guarantee of recovery. Every reader of this book is likely to know of cases of the most devout and faithful saints whose faith displayed itself in accepting that recovery was not for them within God's plan, and whose devotion to Christ was at times challenged but undisturbed. One of those whose writings, coming as they did out of the crucible of pain, have helped so many sufferers, Amy Carmichael of Dohnavur, always refused to pray for healing for herself. As she says, in *Rose from Brier*,[1] she left this to those who loved her. Yet in the early days of her experience as a missionary in South India, she herself used the ministry of laying on of hands in many remarkable instances, only ceasing this method when professional medical assistance was added to her staff. But of Amy Carmichael's saintliness and faith noone who knew her ever had any doubt whatever. Her faith did not cure her, but it was the means of her triumphant endurance during twenty years of pain. More people, one is sure, learned of the deep things of God through the way she bore her suffering than would have done had she remained in full health and activity.

Dr. Leslie Weatherhead has an excellent chapter devoted to the place of faith in healing in his book *Psychology, Religion and Healing*.[2] He draws attention to the fact that the really important question is not whether a patient has faith, but what that faith consists of. Is it a naïve belief, encouraged possibly by certain teaching on the subject, that he is bound to get well? Or is it faith, not in a cure, but in God Himself? Faith in recovery may be simply a form of suggestibility, and be brought about by the fame of the doctor or the hospital, or by the reputation of the healer. It may very often be inspired by a fear of pain, an unwillingness to suffer, or a restless desire to be up and about. Are these very splendid types of faith? It is an understandable and natural human reaction to long to be spared pain, but is it not often horribly tainted with selfishness? Is not even the determination to live because life can be so lovely, far from a deeply Christian faith, however much it may reinforce the will of the patient?

[1] p. 45.   [2] Section VI, Chapter 1.

The cry of earth's anguish went up unto God,
  'Lord, take away pain!
The shadow that darkens the world Thou hast made;
  The close-coiling chain
That strangles the heart: the burden that weighs
  On the wings that would soar.
Lord, take away pain from the world Thou hast made,
  That it love Thee the more!'

Then answered the Lord to the world He had made:
  'Shall I take away pain;
And with it the power of the soul to endure,
  Made strong by the strain?
Shall I take away pity, that knits heart to heart,
  And sacrifice high?
Will you lose all your heroes that lift from the flame
  White brows to the sky?
Shall I take away love that redeems with a price?
  And smiles through the loss?
Can ye spare from the lives that would climb unto Mine
  The Christ on His Cross?'

No, the faith that brings us nearest to the heart of God, that seems to share the nature of Christ Himself, is the faith that says to almighty God, 'Thy will be done', and then accepts whatever happens in utter and complete confidence in the goodness of God. For reasons which we shall try to see as this theme develops, it is not possible to say that God always wants His children to be insulated from suffering. He whose destiny was the cross, and who expected His followers to bear a cross, is hardly likely to guarantee us freedom from pain of some kind—and actual physical pain is the least of all pains. Mental torture can be far harder to explain or to bear. But of whatever kind the suffering may be, if we are pre-armed with more than a superficial faith in God, we shall be enabled to say: 'I want no explanation, only the strength to remain trusting.' Bishop Moule, in his commentary on a passage in Paul's letter to the Christians at Philippi (ii. 30), says, 'Let them look with great simplicity in humble faith for the healing power of their Lord . . . Faith can breathe its most absolute and restful reliance into "IF it be thy will".'

CHAPTER VII

THE PAIN GOD IS ALLOWED TO GUIDE

IN his memorable poem, 'A Sermon', Studdert Kennedy, writing in the throes and agonies of war with its fearful harvest of mutilations and miseries, castigates the easy cant which suggests that broken hearts and bodies can be the will of God and which calls on sufferers to bow before the decrees of God as they fall in judgment on them. If we claim, as we do, that there is a bright side to the existence of pain, we must at the same time be scrupulously careful, in dealing with so solemn a subject, not to indulge in cant. But when people are clamouring to see light, we cannot deny it to them because of the risk that they may think it comes too easily. At the risk of being misunderstood by those who are passing through the valley of the shadow, we cannot keep silence. One of our profoundest Christian poets was reflecting experience of a New Testament character when he wrote—

> Then, welcome each rebuff
> That turns earth's smoothness rough,
> Each sting that bids nor sit nor stand but go!
> Be our joys three-parts pain!
> Strive, and hold cheap the strain;
> Learn, nor account the pang; dare, never grudge
> the throe!

It is not easy to welcome into our life those things that spoil its joys, but Robert Browning knew, what a pampered generation would like to forget, that life is made up as much of what we must endure as of what we can enjoy, and that enjoyment shows up in relief against a sombre background and is greatly enhanced thereby. Thomas Carlyle was, in his own inimitable way, trying to emphasize the same hard-learned truth in his famous passage in *Sartor Resartus* : 'What is this that, ever since earliest years, thou hast been fretting and fuming, and lamenting and self-tormenting, on account of? Say it in a word : is it not because thou art not HAPPY? Because the Thou (sweet gentleman) is not sufficiently honoured,

nourished, soft-bedded, and lovingly cared for? Foolish
soul!'

When we speak of enjoyment, we must, as we saw in
the first chapter, carefully distinguish it from happiness.
Happiness is generally understood to be freedom from
sadness, discomfort or affliction. As such it is a fitful thing,
pausing for the passing moment with the charm of a
butterfly to beautify the scene, but off again to settle elsewhere before long. How we love and cherish the memory
of such moments,—the joys of family life, the beauties of
nature freshly unveiled, the treasures of new vision, the
wonder of science, the insight of great literature, the inspiration of music and art! Our lives are greatly enriched
by such good gifts of God; and if 'the greatest happiness
for the greatest number' were really the supreme good,
then indeed we might rightly complain that these glimpses
of heaven are not more generously bestowed on us.

But who says that happiness is the supreme good? Certainly not Jesus Christ. To Him virtue was God's chief
concern. The inner personality, the characteristics shown
in daily life, the thoughts of the mind and attitude of the
heart : these are the things that matter most. It was for
the character not the comfort of men that Christ went to
the cross. And when we have said that, we are reminded
that the Greek word *charaktēr* means an engraving
tool. In the forming of character the heavenly Sculptor
makes marks on the souls on whom He is working, and
this often hurts. Samuel Rutherford, one of Scotland's
greatest Reformation saints, who only escaped martyrdom in 1661 by dying before it could be carried out, has
left behind him in his letters glimpses of spiritual insight,
written in his own dramatic manner, which take his
readers to the deep places of thought. Writing from a
heart torn by the loss of his wife and two of his children,
a life frustrated by exile and imprisonment at his Bishop's
command, this one-time Professor, Principal and Rector
of St. Andrews University could submit in his ignominy
to the overruling hand of God, and pray, 'Lord cut, Lord
carve, Lord mould, Lord do anything that may perfect
thy Father's image in us and make us meet for glory.'
This was no masochistic self-torture, but a supreme desire
to become the best for God. To him every pain whether

of mind or body was part of the process by which his loving Father shaped his character, and was therefore to be welcomed. Similarly, John Milton, totally blind at the age of forty-four and later bereft of his wife, could write, in his famous Ode, of his

> Soul more bent
> To serve therewith my Maker.

Even Christ Himself was made 'perfect through suffering' (Heb. ii. 10). It seems that in all our Lord's sinless humanity there were yet traits of character which could only be drawn out through experiences of pain. If this was so with the Son of man, how much greater a place is the pain of God's engraving tool likely to have in the perfecting of the souls of men!

There are a number of ways in which it is possible to see the value of pain, though none of these suggest that it is ever less than unpleasant, and on the unenlightened human level, most unwelcome. But the thoughtful Christian realizes, for example, that pain can certainly be a good thing when it is a warning. It sends a man to the dentist and thereby prevents further decay and worse trouble. The discomfort of first being drunk keeps many a man from falling again. The fear of pain stops children from adventuring beyond reasonable limits. In the realm of the spirit the same thing is often true. Calamity and disaster have frequently been a warning to the careless and many examples could be given of those to whom God has spoken at such times. Indeed, C. S. Lewis, in his thoughtful treatise *The Problem of Pain*, argues that there are some people who will never listen to God until something terrible happens. They are not interested enough to hear God's still small voice in the quiet, so He speaks to them more loudly. Dr. Lewis calls pain 'God's megaphone to rouse a deaf world'.[1] He goes on to acknowledge his own tendency, which is surely shared by us all, to copy the puppy dog which after its bath delights to revert to rolling in the dust. We are so earthbound by nature that when all goes well with us and life is free of tribulation we live happily independent of God. It is suffering that comes to warn us of the imminent danger of

---

[1] p. 81.

this self-sufficiency and to turn us back to God. Robert
Louis Stevenson, on his 'dim inglorious battlefield of bed
and physic-bottle', spoke from the depths of a personal
experience which was to grow more acute as the years
went on of his need to be roused to reality by God in the
only way that would work with him, through the kindly
hurt of the 'Celestial Surgeon' :

> If I have faltered more or less
> In my great task of happiness;
> If I have moved among my race
> And shown no glorious morning face;
> If beams from happy human eyes
> Have moved me not; if morning skies,
> Books, and my food, and summer rain
> Knocked on my sullen heart in vain:—
> Lord, thy most pointed pleasure take
> And stab my spirit broad awake;
> Or, Lord, if too obdurate I,
> Choose thou, before that spirit die,
> A piercing pain, a killing sin,
> And to my dead heart run them in!

As Hezekiah said, after his recovery from a serious illness
which he had fully expected to be fatal, 'Lo, it was for
my welfare that I had great bitterness' (Is. xxxviii. 17).

Dr. Paul Tournier, whose book *A Doctor's Casebook*
throws so much scriptural light on the question of suffering, quotes one of Pascal's prayers, 'Thou didst give me
health that I might serve Thee, and I put it all to worldly
use. Now Thou sendest me sickness to correct me; let me
not use it to avoid Thee through my impatience.' He goes
on to call suffering 'a school of faith'. There is indeed
much in the Bible to lead us to regard it as a form of
spiritual discipline, a chastening which we are to welcome
for the good of our souls. Eliphaz may have been com-
placent in his preaching contentment to Job when he
pointed this out, but his words are echoed in many other
places in the biblical record. 'Behold, happy is the man
whom God reproves; therefore despise not the chastening of the Almighty. For he wounds, but he binds up; he
smites, but his hands heal' (Jb. v. 17, 18). The writer to
the Hebrews enlarged on this same theme as he travelled
in thought from the faithful endurance of the saints

(chapter xi) to the sufferings of Christ, and the fact that to follow the Crucified is to benefit from His chastening hand : 'Have you forgotten the exhortation which addresses you as sons?—"My son, do not regard lightly the discipline of the Lord, nor lose courage when you are punished by him. For the Lord disciplines him whom he loves, and chastises every son whom he receives." It is for discipline that you have to endure. God is treating you as sons; for what son is there whom his father does not discipline? If you are left without discipline, in which all have participated, then you are illegitimate children and not sons. Besides this, we have had earthly fathers to discipline us and we respected them. Shall we not much more be subject to the Father of spirits and live? For they disciplined us for a short time at their pleasure, but *he disciplines us for our good*, that we may share his holiness. For the moment all discipline seems painful rather than pleasant; later it yields the peaceful fruit of righteousness to those who have been trained by it. Therefore lift your drooping hands and strengthen your weak knees . . .' (Heb. xii. 5–12). No-one can read these strong words without feeling that here is a sound and healthy outlook on suffering as a form of chastening which is guaranteed to cure us of being 'faint-hearted' (verse 3) or weak-kneed !

Chastisement or discipline is not really the same as punishment. We have already seen that there is no scriptural authority for saying that we suffer as a punishment for our sins in any exact sense (though this may sometimes be so, in which case we believe that God makes it clear to us). Chastisement is more of the order of corrective training, 'for our profit, that we might be partakers of his holiness' (AV). One can think of parallels, admittedly very imperfect, in the relationships of teacher to pupil and parent to child in ordinary society. The Bible teaches us that God does, on occasion, 'use' suffering, even perhaps we can sometimes say 'send' it; certainly He allows it as a corrective. Our word 'tribulation' is derived from the *tribulum*, the Roman farmers' threshing instrument whereby the grain was separated from the husk, a painful process, could the wheat but speak. A common New Testament word, usually translated 'tribulation', mean in the Greek 'pressure' such as might involve being crushed to death. Many modern circumstances provide suffering of this kind : it may be pressures on the mind and heart; strains on the nerves; or some crushing weight on the emotional life. These are all hard to bear, but no Christian can deny that such things have an important part to play in the proper development of his character, and perhaps a truer appreciation of his sins. When our forefathers said of their troubles that 'these things are sent to try us', they were not far wrong. God has a father's watchful eye on his children for their ultimate good within his loving purposes. We can be sure that it does not come easily to Him to give His children pain, but often there is no other way of helping us.

Out of the miseries of their captivity in alien Babylon, the prophet expresses amongst his people's lamentations this vision of their probable significance and eventual end : 'Though he (the Lord) cause grief, he will have compassion according to the abundance of his steadfast love; for he does not willingly afflict or grieve the sons of men . . . Let us test and examine our ways, and return to the Lord !' (La. iii. 32, 33, 40). Writing from the lonely experiences of exile on the island of Patmos, the aged apostle John looks back on the ways of God, and similarly sees something of the meaning of the things God's people are called upon to endure. 'Those whom I love, I reprove and chasten; so be zealous and repent' (Rev. iii. 19). Both Old and New Testament writers have not a shred of doubt about the divine love which lies behind their pains, and only urge their people to recognize this and turn back in penitence to God.

We cannot forget that though Job suffered in innocence, yet the experiences which he went through led him to personal repentance, and a fresher and clearer vision of his God than he had ever had before. His wonderful story comes to an end with his answer to the Lord, 'I know that . . . no purpose of thine can be thwarted . . . I had heard of thee by the hearing of the ear, but now my eye sees thee; therefore I despise myself, and repent in dust and ashes' (Jb. xlii. 2, 5, 6).

We find in some biblical writers the analogy of something like Tennyson's furnace, where the 'iron dug from central gloom' is

> heated hot with burning fears
> And dipped in baths of hissing tears,
> And battered with the shocks of doom
> To shape and use.

For instance, God's prophet speaks thus of His relations with His people : 'I have tried you in the furnace of affliction' (Is. xlviii. 10). Malachi represented God as a refiner of silver using the pain of fiery trial to purge out the dross and leave a purified remainder, which would then be better fitted to 'present right offerings to the Lord' (iii. 2, 3). The writer of the apocryphal book Wisdom describes the sufferings of his people in the same way. 'Having borne a little chastening, they shall receive great good; because God made trial of them, and found them worthy of himself. As gold in the furnace he proved them, and as a whole burnt offering he accepted them' (iii. 5, 6). Peter called on his fellow-sufferers to rejoice, 'though now for a little while you may have to suffer various trials, so that the genuineness of your faith, more precious than gold which though perishable is tested by fire, may redound to praise and glory and honour at the revelation of Jesus Christ' (1 Pet. i. 6, 7). In the process of refining our faith and character until only that which is durable and genuine remains, there is bound to be the element of pain. But the result of such chastening and discipline must be a closer approximation to what God would have us to be. Miss Amy Carmichael, in her book written specially for sufferers, tells how she asked her South Indian village goldsmith when he knew his metal was really purified. He replied, 'When I can see my face in it.' [1] Would that God could see even the dimmest reflection of His likeness in those lives which He honours with the discipline of refinement!

Much of the process of soul-refining involves learning the meaning of obedience. We read of Jesus that, 'although he was a Son, he learned obedience through what he suffered' (Heb. v. 8). If Christ, the Son of God, who never at any time offended against His Father, had need to learn the manner and degree of necessary obedi-

[1] *Rose from Brier*, p. 29.

ence to the will of God, how much more true it is of us! Soren Kierkegaard, writing from a heart torn by personal conflict and pain, has a wonderful passage about the obedience of Christ in his profound work *Gospel of Sufferings*.[1] He brings it to a head with the suggestion that the true obedience of man to God can only be learned in the school of suffering. 'He who was and who is the Truth, he who knew all yet learned one thing, and nothing else, learned obedience by the things which he suffered. Were it possible that a man should learn obedience to God apart from sufferings, then Christ, as man, had not needed to learn it from sufferings. It was human obedience that he learned from sufferings, for the eternal accord of his will with that of the Father is certainly not obedience. Obedience belongs to his humiliation, as it is written, "he humbled himself and became obedient."'

There are endless lessons that can be learned in perhaps no other school than suffering. The kind of education in which the pupil becomes a law to himself and discipline is at a discount, has no authority in Scripture, and is utterly unlike the ways of God with men. If Keats was right when, in writing to Fanny Brawne, he called this world 'the vale of soul making', he no doubt was thinking of the hard work and much pain and discomfort involved in the process of finding one's way to the ultimate end of that formidable valley. 'Blessed are those', cries the Psalmist, 'who going through the vale of misery use it for a well' (lxxxiv. 6, PBV). Instead of miserably dwelling on the tearful aspect of life in this troublesome world, the man who knows that God loves him, and whose faith rests in that knowledge, can turn his passage through this dark valley into the happy process whereby he emerges at the end purified of much that is unworthy, and nearer to the God who has done so much for him.

If we believe that our loving God and heavenly Father is also the God of holiness and truth we must expect, in His dealings with His children, beauty of character to be the first essential. This means that what happens *in* us is much more important than what happens *to* us. As we have seen, the writer to the Hebrews is bold enough to assert that by the many sufferings that came His way,

[1] Chapter 3.

leading up to 'the suffering of death', Jesus Himself was 'made perfect' (Heb. ii. 10). We are surely to understand by the word 'perfection' in this setting, full spiritual maturity. In the experience of Jesus, part of the process of growth to greater perfection lay through the impact of pain and trouble upon Him. Peter hints at the same truth in relation to Christian believers when he prays that the God, who has all the grace we need, 'after you have suffered a little while . . . will himself restore, establish, and strengthen you' (1 Pet. v. 10). He does not specify here whether he has physical suffering in mind, as he has in the previous chapter, or whether he is thinking of the mental and spiritual conflicts, the pains of which he knew so well in his own life, and to which he refers in this context. But the principle remains the same : the tree sends its roots deeper the more the wind tears at its branches, and the deeper the roots grow, the more fruitful the tree. Some of the greatest men of history have been like Wordsworth's Happy Warrior,

> more able to endure,
> As more exposed to suffering and distress.

Beethoven, stricken down with a deafness that killed the world of sound for him, refused to be overcome, but used this awful handicap to stimulate his imagination, and many of his most triumphant works are the fruit of this deeper genius. Rembrandt began to show far greater depth of insight in his later paintings after the tragedies of his bankruptcy and loneliness had driven him back to serious biblical themes, a very different soul from the cheerful man-about-town whose portrait of himself dangling Saskia on his knee betrays his earlier *bonhomie*.

To those who look to the formation of Christian character as the most vitally significant thing in their lives, it is not difficult to say with the Psalmist, 'Before I was afflicted I went astray . . . it is good for me that I was afflicted' (Ps. cxix. 67, 71). Kierkegaard, in his sermon on Matthew xi. 30 ('My yoke is easy, and my burden is light') takes the Greek word *chrēstos* ('easy' or 'good') and argues from this that for the Christian any trouble shared under the yoke of Christ is bound to be beneficial, and therefore must be welcomed. 'There is one thought and only one

which has the power of transforming by faith the heavy
burden into a burden that is light, and this thought is that
it is good, that the heavy burden is good for one. But that
the heavy suffering is good is something that must be
believed because it cannot be seen. Perhaps we can see
afterwards that it *has been* good, but at the time of suffering we can neither see it, nor, even though ever so many
people with the best motives keep on repeating it, can we
hear it spoken; it must be believed.' [1] There are many, as
we have seen, who teach that the work of faith is to believe
that deliverance from pain is God's obvious will for mankind. It is surely a profounder faith that we find in this
Danish philosopher's insight; a vision of truth which
came to him not only from a study of the Scriptures, but
also in the pains of his own experience. He was the son
of an old man and suffered all his life from an almost
pathological sensitivity, leading him to phases of morbid
introspection, all of which eventually led to the breaking
of his engagement to a charming young girl, which in turn
only added to his misery. 'From earliest time I have been
nailed fast to one or another suffering to the very verge of
insanity . . . From a child I was in the power of a pro-
digious melancholy.' Yet his faith held him through the
tortures of his suffering, and he believed it had all been
for his good.

Similarly, in his book *Miraculous Healing*, Dr. H. W.
Frost writes of a man who said to him, 'Health is the best
thing in the world—except sickness!' 'Indeed,' he goes on,
'knowing what God has done for me through physical
weakness, and being persuaded that certain blessings
could never have been given to me in any other way than
through such an experience, I feel that it would have been
nothing short of a calamity to have missed the physical
suffering through which I have passed' [2]; to which many
of us would say a hearty Amen! For 'It is a blessed fever
that fetcheth Christ to the bedside', as Rutherford
quaintly expressed it.

For the less committed Christian, or for those who
have not yet allowed the troubles God permits to do what
He has planned for them, suffering still is a good thing,
an essential means of grace. Paul in his letter to Corinth

[1] *Gospel of Sufferings*, p. 32. [2] p. 38.

reminds his readers of how pain can bring men to God, even the pain of a severe letter, which he had felt he must write to them, and which had caused them considerable hurt. 'Your pain induced you to repent. For you were pained as God meant you to be pained, and so you got no harm from what I did; the pain God is allowed to guide ends in a saving repentance never to be regretted, whereas the world's pain ends in death' (2 Cor. vii. 9, 10, Moffatt). In these words, *'the pain God is allowed to guide'*, we seem to have the clue to how and why suffering can often be a blessing. Let us seek the reason behind our troubles; let us realize that God is over all and wants to turn our pain into good; let us submit to His will and allow Him the freedom in our experiences which He will need to guide our pain along the channels best fitted to meet our need. In this spirit of willing submission that great German Christian leader, Dietrich Bonhoeffer, sent a poem with his last message from the Gestapo prison in Berlin during the heavy raids of 1945. He was executed on April 9th, 1945, a few days before the liberation by the Allies of the concentration camp to which he had been transferred. He leaves the issue of his sufferings entirely in the hands of his Father in heaven to whom he had long ago dedicated his whole life :—

> Should it be ours to drain the cup of grieving
> even to the dregs of pain, at thy command,
> we will not falter, thankfully receiving
> all that is given by thy loving hand.
>
> But, should it be thy will once more to release us
> to life's enjoyment and its good sunshine,
> that we've learned from sorrow shall increase us
> and all our life be dedicate as thine.[1]

[1] *The Cost of Discipleship*, p. 17.

bitterness. Nowhere in the long Passion story do we find
that note of resentment or rebellion which is the first
reaction of the ordinary man in such circumstances.
    There are, however, many who, while admitting that it
cannot
God when
Instead we find them seeking various means of escape.

CHAPTER VIII

SUFFERING NOT A PROBLEM,
AN OPPORTUNITY

JUST as it is possible, by setting the sails correctly, to
    travel fast and securely into the wind, or alternatively
    to allow the wind to take control and drive one in the
    opposite direction, so, in relation to the onslaught of
suffering, more depends on the attitude we adopt towards
it than on its own particular vigour or vehemence. The
same affliction can affect two people in quite different
ways, according to the manner in which they face it. Now
it is vital to remember that whatever attitude is taken up
it will be the fruit of the faith of the individual, formed,
probably, in calmer times, but firm by the time the trouble
comes. That is why there is real value in considering the
subject of pain, even when life seems singularly free from
it, for no-one can tell when the break may come.

One of the commonest reactions to trouble is a bitter
resentment, a whining complaint that this is unfair, that
God is dealing unjustly with one. 'The Almighty has dealt
very bitterly with me', cried Naomi on her return home
to Bethlehem, bereft of her husband and two sons, her
sufferings leaving such a mark upon her that her friends
said : 'Is this Naomi?', to which she replied : 'Call
me Mara' (the embittered one) (Ru. i. 19, 20). Before we
criticize her too much for her harsh judgment on God's
dealings with her we should ask ourselves if we never rebel
at injustices, unfair treatment, disappointments and such
like, which, while not perhaps taking the form of physical
suffering, yet in principle are part and parcel of the hardship which God allows to come our way. Was anyone
more unjustly treated than our Lord Himself, and yet of
Him we read that He found delight in doing God's will,
and 'for the joy that was set before him endured the cross'
(Heb. xii. 2). We know in what an unimaginable mental
struggle Jesus was involved on the level of His human
reluctance to go to Calvary, yet in the end the will of God
became the cup He was prepared to drink in spite of its

bitterness. Nowhere in the long Passion story do we find that note of resentment or rebellion which is the first reaction of the ordinary man in such circumstances.

There are, however, many who, while admitting that it cannot be right to harden one's heart in rebellion against God when trouble comes, yet do not readily accept it. Instead we find them seeking various means of escape. There is an illustration of this longing to escape from, rather than face up to, trouble in one of David's Psalms where, in a moment of despair (during the apparent desertion and treachery of a friend), he cries out 'My heart is sore pained within me : and the terrors of death are fallen upon me. Fearfulness and trembling are come upon me, and horror hath overwhelmed me. And I said, Oh that I had wings like a dove ! *For then would I fly away, and be at rest . . . I would hasten my escape from the windy storm and tempest*' (Ps. lv. 4–8, AV). There is not one of us who cannot sympathize with this longing. We all have phases of wishing there were some place or sphere where we could get away from our circumstances and find untrammelled peace, like Gerard Manley Hopkins' nun, whose longing to find a haven in taking the veil was really a kind of escapism :

> I have desired to go
> Where springs not fail,
> To fields where flies no sharp and sided hail
> And a few lilies blow.
>
> And I have asked to be
> Where no storms come,
> Where the green swell is in the havens dumb,
> And out of the swing of the sea.

But, at once, we realize this is the wish of the coward. Character is not formed in the hectic rush of escapism. Trouble avoided means further trouble met in another direction. We cannot and must not try to escape. Psychologically it is fatal. Spiritually it is the admission of failure. And this is what David eventually realized, for in a later Psalm written during the same era of Absalom's rebellion and David's exile, he rises to much greater heights of faith. 'My soul trusteth in thee : yea, in the shadow of thy wings will I make my refuge, until these calamities be overpast' (Ps. lvii. 1, AV). Here David has substituted for the mythical wings of an escaping dove, the overshadowing protection and strength of the wings of a merciful God who is ready to shelter him. In quiet trust he is now prepared to wait, through the troubles of the time, until God shall see fit to bring him deliverance. He is no longer praying 'O God spare me', but 'O God shelter me'. To such an extent has his faith taken him, as it can also take us. Far short though it comes, it reminds us of Jesus' sublime courage when, knowing all that was waiting for Him in Jerusalem (Mt. xvii. 22, 23), knowing that His followers would fight for Him and all the hosts of heaven could hasten His escape if He asked them (Jn. xviii. 36; Mt. xxvi. 53), He yet steadfastly 'set his face to go to Jerusalem' (Lk. ix. 51). There on the cross, with a courage in suffering that led to mankind's salvation, He even refused the pain-killing drug which would have eased His last hour.

Both to rebel against God, and to seek to escape out of our difficulties are unworthy of the Christian. It is equally wrong for us so to dwell upon our troubles that we get bogged down in self-pity and self-commiseration. If we allow this to happen, it will not be long before we shall find ourselves thinking, and possibly saying, 'No-one ever suffered quite so much as I have. It's one thing after another. I must be made for this.' The supreme example of this in literature is surely Mrs. Gummidge (of Dickens' *David Copperfield*), who used to burst into tears when the fire smoked, or the potatoes got burnt, saying, 'I'm a lone, lorn creetur, everythink goes contrairy with me.' In spite of having the most comfortable chair and the warmest place by the fire, she constantly complained that the cold gave her 'the creeps', and when told that others often felt cold too, her reply was to the effect that 'I feel it more'. When Mr. Peggotty slapped her on the back to cheer her up (the worst possible treatment for melancholics) she drew out a black hankie to wipe her eyes, and kept it ready on her knees.

While we all recognize the degree of satire in Dickens' portrait, and the pathological state which Mrs. Gummidge had reached, yet there is enough truth in his picture to make many of us conscious of how near we often are to pitying ourselves. There are some people who would rather be told : 'How tired you are looking', than : 'I've never seen you look better'. There are many who are not quite truthful when they say, 'I've not had a wink of sleep', or 'I'm a martyr to corns', and are in danger of enjoying their ill health because it gives them a splendid opportunity of wallowing in the warmth of soft sympathy. Is anything more weakening than this? Is anything more diametrically opposed to the spirit of Jesus? It is impossible to imagine Him exaggerating His troubles, or seeking the weakening sympathy of others. When He began to warn His disciples that He was going to a cruel end (Mt. xvi. 21-25), Peter, in the natural spontaneity of a friendship that wanted to save his friend from pain, besought Jesus with the words, 'Pity thyself, Lord' (marginal reading). Whereupon Jesus, with unexpected severity, turned on him and rebuked him as an instrument of Satan for displaying a totally human attitude when he should have been godly enough to 'trace the rainbow through the rain' and see our Lord's sufferings *sub specie aeternitatis*. This led Jesus immediately to remind them of what He had several times mentioned before (Lk. ix. 23, xiv. 27), that if they were to belong to Him they must be prepared for self-denial, not self-pity; a cross to carry, not a cushion to recline upon. And He lived out what He was saying when, as He literally stumbled under the weight of His own cross, He turned to the women around, who could hardly bear to watch His agonies any longer, and said to them, 'Do not weep for me.'

Amy Carmichael, who, as we have seen, had so many years of weakening pain, confesses in one of her books her temptation to be sorry for herself and the challenge that came to her as she remembered the endurance and discipline required in mountain climbing. 'Let us face it now,' she writes. 'Which is harder, to be well and doing things, or to be ill and bearing things? It was a long time before I saw the comfort in that question. Here we may find our opportunity to crucify that cowardly thing, the softness that would sink to things below, self-pity, dullness, selfishness, ungrateful gloom.' The harder way is likelier to be God's way, for it cures us of the desire to be pampered and spoilt, and leads us on to higher levels still.

What then is our attitude to be? Are we simply to grin and bear our troubles with a calm kind of resignation, and

> Wish the long unhappy dream would end,
> And waive all claim to bliss, and try to bear
> With close-lipped patience for our only friend?

Is the height of faith represented by acknowledging our 'bad luck' and setting ourselves stoically to shoulder it? This may be so in the case of the average man judging a situation without any reference to the Christian revelation, as if there had never been a Christ on a cross. The history of the world is full of cases, which we cannot but admire, of those who have steeled themselves to face pain (of whatever kind) without flinching. In such an instance, courage triumphs, but faith is limited. These are the kind of people who sigh deeply, and then say quietly, 'God's will be done.' We acknowledge their bravery and respect their lack of resentment, escapism or self-pity. But the Christian knows there is a still higher way. He knows there was something more than resignation in the life of Jesus. He notices that after the awful hours of agony in the garden of Gethsemane, when at last Jesus had found Himself able to accept the cup from His Father's hand and say 'not my will, but thine, be done', He wakes His disciples with the words, 'Rise, let us be going' (Mt. xxvi. 44–46). He then goes out to meet God's will, even though it comes to Him in the shape of an armed gang led by a traitor friend. For Jesus, suffering was not a problem but an opportunity, not something merely to be undergone, but something to be used for God. And so He met His sufferings and converted them to the eternal blessing of the world. He did not just bear His sufferings, He transformed them.

If, as we have seen, it is wrong to face trouble with the frown of resentment, a rush to escape, moans of self-pity or even the sigh of resignation, what should a Christian, following our Lord's example and drawing on the grace of God to an extent that others do not, be expected to do? The first step is quietly to accept what comes as being allowed of God, and within the orbit of His providence. There are many examples of this in the Scriptures: Aaron, after the sudden death of his two sons in mysterious circumstances, 'held his peace' (Lv. x. 3); Eli, hearing of the judgment of God through the lips of the child Samuel, accepted it with the words, 'It is the Lord; let him do what seems good to him' (1 Sa. iii. 18); the woman of Shunem, who suddenly lost her much-prayed-for son, greeted the prophet Elisha's messenger with words of more significance than mere eastern politeness, saying, 'It is well' (2 Ki. iv. 26). In the words of Amy Carmichael : 'In acceptance lieth peace.' By this she means not a mild acquiescence in the state of ill health or trouble or whatever it may be, but 'contentment with the unexplained', due to a deep-seated faith in the loving providence of God. In a moment of deep bereavement, when one who was not only a very close personal friend but also an almost indispensable colleague in their lonely missionary work in South India died, this word set itself into poetry :

> He said, 'I will forget the dying faces;
> The empty places—
> They shall be filled again;
> O voices mourning deep within me, cease.'
> Vain, vain the word : vain, vain :
> Not in forgetting lieth peace.
>
> He said, 'I will crowd action upon action,
> The strife of faction
> Shall stir my spirit to flame;
> O tears that drown the fire of manhood, cease.'
> Vain, vain the word; vain, vain :
> Not in endeavour lieth peace.
>
> He said, 'I will withdraw me and be quiet,
> Why meddle in life's riot?
> Shut be my door to pain.
> Desire, thou dost befool me, thou shalt cease.'
> Vain, vain the word : vain, vain :
> Not in aloofness lieth peace.
>
> He said, 'I will submit; I am defeated;
> God hath depleted
> My life of its rich gain.
> O futile murmurings; why will ye not cease?'
> Vain, vain the word; vain, vain :
> Not in submission lieth peace.

He said, 'I will accept the breaking sorrow
Which God to-morrow
Will to His son explain.'
Then did the turmoil deep within him cease.
Not vain the word, not vain:
For in acceptance lieth peace.

It is interesting to notice that in that book *Margaret*, which we have already mentioned, the turning-point in the young girl's spiritual experience came when she was told how serious her illness was, and the likelihood that she had only a few more months to live. Her great friend who writes her story, and who was himself led to Christ by her example, tells of the manner of her acceptance of this death-sentence. 'Tranquility, a sense of humour that never deserted her, and a quality that was more than radiance were hers. They shone in her eyes and face as I sat with her now—five minutes from being told she must die . . . "If He thinks it best, He'll heal me; if not, well, I know it will be what He thinks is right. I can do whatever that is, Jim!" And frequently as the end drew near she kept repeating "I wouldn't change anything".' [1]

That sublime, profound yet child-like trust of Margaret's is found in the life and experience of Paul. We deduce from several hints in his writings that he had suffered for a long time from some physical handicap which was intensely trying in itself, and which seriously handicapped his work for God. This affliction has been variously thought to be ophthalmia, epilepsy or lameness. He uses strong words to describe it, so it must have been very severe. 'A stake driven through my flesh' is how Dr. Way translates the phrase. Weymouth uses the word 'agony' for the apparently constant nagging infuriation of this thing. 'A thorn was given me in the flesh,' Paul writes, 'a messenger of Satan, to harass me, to keep me from being too elated. Three times I besought the Lord about this, that it should leave me; but he said to me, "My grace is sufficient for you, for my power is made perfect in weakness." I will all the more gladly boast of my weaknesses, that the power of Christ may rest upon me. For the sake of Christ, then, I am content with weaknesses,

[1] pp. 60, 62.

insults, hardships, persecutions, and calamities; for when I am weak, then I am strong' (2 Cor. xii. 7–10).

Paul was convinced that Satan was trying to bring him low by an attack on his physical health. Knowing that all things, even the works of the devil, were ultimately a matter for the Lord's overriding sovereignty to deal with, he prayed on three occasions to be set free from this thing. The Lord's reply was not to take it from him, but to remind him that the grace of the Lord was able to help him face and overcome it, for 'in the forge of infirmity strength is wrought to perfection' (Way). In words which have been an untold inspiration since to everyone who has relied upon them, Paul was able to say 'for the sake of Christ, ... I am content with calamities', because he had learned that 'My grace is sufficient for you'. Spurgeon tells somewhere the story of how he was feeling depressed and disheartened at one point in his ministry when he saw from his study chair these words framed and hanging on the wall. He had seen them many times before, but just now he sat and gazed on them seeking to grasp the truth they stood for. After a while he thought he saw the word 'My' growing larger and larger and the word 'thee' getting smaller and smaller, until it dawned on him that whatever one's pains or troubles may be, they are not all that large, and there is no limit to the extent that we can call on the grace of God to help us meet them.

Paul, then, met his problem by accepting the fact that it was not God's will for this affliction to be taken from him. He did more; he went on to turn this natural disappointment into an opportunity for rejoicing. Listen to the note of infectious Christian faith and courage which on different occasions he shares with his fellow Christians: 'I am filled with comfort. With all our affliction, I am overjoyed' (2 Cor. vii. 4). 'I rejoice in my sufferings for your sake' (Col. i. 24). 'You received the word in much affliction, with joy inspired by the Holy Spirit' (1 Thes. i. 6). Very few of us can welcome our troubles in the way Paul seems to have done, turning his weakness of body into strength of character, but with his example before us, and the same grace of God at our disposal, we should do no less. When we can accept, even welcome, our 'infirmities, reproaches, necessities, persecutions and distresses' as Paul did for Christ's sake, and make them an opportunity for glorifying God, we shall have discovered the first secret of how to turn suffering from an intractable problem into an inspiring opportunity.

An essential part of the quiet acceptance of suffering is an accompanying confidence in God. This trust shows itself in taking an unanswered prayer such as Paul's and, instead of arguing about it, and perhaps searching for some hidden reason why it was not answered by deliverance as he had hoped, using it as a means of strengthening our faith. So Oswald Chambers says of Job, 'I trust one whose character I know, but whose ways are hidden in mystery.' William Cowper, writing from the depths of a melancholia from which he would have given his right hand to be delivered, wrote how

> Blind unbelief is sure to err,
> And scan His work in vain;
> God is His own interpreter,
> And He will make it plain.

Cowper still believed in God and His power to work wonders. Job's faith in God was such as to carry him to the point where, even if his ill-health were to be fatal, he still would end his painful days with an undiminished trust. The prophet of Israel's decline, pouring out his lament at the collapse of his people and the terrible atrocities committed by the victorious Chaldeans, still retained a flicker of hope as he recalled the mercies of the Lord. 'Remember my affliction and my bitterness, the wormwood and the gall! My soul continually thinks of it and is bowed down within me. But this I call to mind, and therefore I have hope : The steadfast love of the Lord never ceases, his mercies never come to an end; they are new every morning; great is thy faithfulness' (La. iii. 19–23). Nothing more surely cures a man of self-pity than to be taken out of his sufferings by recalling the goodness of God, how much worse things might have been, how God never lets us down, how every day His faithfulness is shown.

For the Christian living in the light of the Bible there is much fuel with which to stoke the fires of faith. In the light of the cross, as we shall see later, in the biographies of the saints before and after Christ, in the promises of God made to and through them, there is enough inspiration to see things in a better light than the world can ever put upon them. The faith of the Christian is stimulated by these insights which enable him to live in the midst of troubles a life of enviable security and trust. For him his faith can turn his troubles from an agonizing mental problem into an opportunity to demonstrate the value of personal confidence in Christ. In his very moving account of how faith sustained his life in a Japanese prisoner-of-war camp,[1] Ken Attiwill shows how Christian faith can shine against a background of awful suffering. He has unsuspectingly rested his shaving-mirror on a sack which conceals the dead body of a fellow-prisoner. 'I suppose it is part of the pattern', he writes. 'There must be more in this humble death than meets the eye. There must be a purpose behind it, or the whole pattern is pointless . . . He has not lived and died in vain—I'll not have it so. He came for a purpose, lived for a purpose, suffered for a purpose, and now has miserably died for a purpose . . . This theory, or knowledge—this alone makes sense of suffering. God requires it. Why? Because suffering humbles the proud heart of mortal man, teaches wisdom in the eternal way of life . . .' Faith like that sustained this man through three and a half years' humiliation, sickness and torture at the hands of the Japanese. Surrounded by men dying in the throes of dysentery, he writes in his secret diary, 'For myself, I'm thrown once more hard upon God's mercy—the only apparent hope of peace whether I live or die. God knows I want to live; but if I have to die, I feel it best to make peace with hope in eternity. What else offers so calm a sense of security as to imagine oneself in the care of an everlasting father, kind and forgiving all the mistakes I've made, one who has already forgiven prodigal sons like me and has a banquet waiting? There is no comparable peace that I know.'

[1] *The Rising Sunset*, pp. 89, 100.

CHAPTER IX

HOW CAN PAIN GLORIFY GOD?

THE fact that suffering, far from being a hindrance to faith in God, can actually be a means of showing His ways with mankind in a new light, is clear throughout the Bible. It was our Lord's own view, and therefore should be ours, that, for instance, even the tragedy of sickness followed by death and bereavement could glorify God. It was hard for the disciples, and next to impossible at the time for his sisters Mary and Martha, to believe that the loss of their brother Lazarus was really, as Jesus said, 'for the glory of God' (Jn. xi. 4). This did not mean, of course, that Mary's tears and Martha's escapism were pleasing to Jesus. It certainly did not mean that He could not feel with them in their natural sorrow, for we read that it was with them that 'Jesus wept'. It means that He knew how the outcome of their immediate sadness would be an ultimate joy leading to increased faith in the power of God, which is exactly what happened. We read that after Lazarus' miraculous deliverance from the tomb, 'many . . . believed' in Jesus (Jn. xi. 45). In this signal demonstration of victory over the grave, Jesus declared that the glory of God could be seen (verse 40). To the followers of the Master, all the passing agony was worth bearing if it meant magnifying the Lord and leading many to faith in Him.

Similarly, on the occasion which we have already considered, when His disciples were asking Jesus about the problem of the innocent sufferer (in this case a man blind from birth), Jesus replied in the same vein. This man's sufferings had been permitted in order that 'the works of God might be made manifest in him' (Jn. ix. 3). When he did miraculously recover his sight, this could only be accounted for on the grounds of Jesus being the Son of God (verses 30–38). The miracle forced this truth upon all who did not deliberately blind themselves to it, and caused them to acknowledge the hand of God in healing the man's blindness contrary to all expectations.

In the realm of the apparently miraculous recovery of the sick which is often associated with 'divine' healing today, there have undoubtedly been many instances which in this way have brought glory to God. There are from time to time cases in which no medical explanation of the phenomena can be found, and few members of the medical profession would deny that remarkable supernatural healing and restoration does occasionally take place. One also hears of other kinds of so-called miracles of healing. It would seem that a good way of judging whether these are the fruit of genuine repentance and faith in Christ, or some fictitious or ephemeral phenomenon, would be, 'Does it bring glory to God?'

But God is not only glorified in spectacular recovery from sickness. He can be glorified quite as effectively by the spirit in which sickness or suffering is faced and borne. In his supremely moving account of the sufferings of South Africa, *Cry the Beloved Country*, Alan Paton makes one of his characters encourage the pathetic priest Kumalo with the words : 'The world is full of trouble . . . I have never thought that a Christian would be free of suffering, for our Lord suffered. And I come to believe that He suffered, not to save us from suffering, but to teach us how to bear suffering. For He knew that there is no life without suffering.'[1] How wonderfully the underprivileged of the earth, like South Africa's dark children, have demonstrated the truth of this word !

On the way to the cross, Jesus said, 'Now must the Son of man be glorified.' Such an ignominious, cruel and shameful death was an altogether 'out of this world' kind of glory. But then that was the kind of person Jesus was. The whole story of our Lord's last sufferings is the tale of God's glory being demonstrated where it had never been seen before, in the torture and death-throes of a Victim of Jewish and Roman persecution outside the Jerusalem city wall. Again, we have already seen how Paul's thorn in the flesh was allowed to remain, and how he recognized this as something to thank God for, a means perhaps of self-humiliation (2 Cor. xii. 7), keeping him in his place lest he should think his visions of God made him out in some way to be privileged above his fellows. Peter also

[1] p. 193.

points out in his first letter that what brought glory to
God was the way in which his readers, when they were
wrongfully accused or attacked, took it all patiently after
the example of Jesus Himself. To them all he wrote, 'In
this you rejoice, though now for a little while you may
have to suffer various trials, so that the genuineness of
your faith . . . *may redound to praise and glory and honour
at the revelation of Jesus Christ*' (1 Pet. i. 6,7). To the converted Christian slaves of pagan masters he said, 'What
credit is it, if when you do wrong and are beaten for it
you take it patiently? But if when you do right and suffer
for it you take it patiently, you have God's approval'
(ii. 20). To those who were haunted by impending persecution and martyrdom, Peter's word was the same.
'Beloved, do not be surprised at the fiery ordeal which
comes upon you to prove you, as though something
strange were happening to you . . . If you are reproached
for the name of Christ, *you are blessed, because the spirit
of glory and of God rests upon you* . . . if one suffers as a
Christian, let him not be ashamed, but *under that name
let him glorify God*' (iv. 12-16).

There is a triumphant spirit running through these New
Testament writings which raises suffering, much of it
severe and most of it unmerited, to a level that gives glory
to God because of the way it is accepted, and allowed to
do its work in the soul. The history of saintliness is the
story of men and women of God whose faith enabled them
to endure and triumph in their sufferings, and thereby be
drawn closer to God and conformed nearer to His perfect
pattern for them. Cardinal Mercier, for example, writing
just before his death, could see his pains in this light, and
read their meaning as a sacrifice to offer to God. 'Today
the doctors tell me that I have a tumour in the stomach.
From the depth of my soul I thank God that I have something to offer him . . . From the beginning of my illness
I have refused to think of praying for my recovery. I leave
myself entirely in the hands of Providence, desiring but
one thing only, that God should draw from my poor self
all the glory that he can, regardless of the cost.' While
few people, perhaps, would go so far as to agree with St.
Hildegard's assertion that 'God does not dwell in healthy
bodies', yet who is to say that this kind of total commit-

ment of a doomed body to God is not just as glorifying to Him as the full and free exercise of one in the peak of health?

One enormous benefit that suffering brings, and a very real means of glorifying God, is the ability of the sufferer to understand, sympathize with and help those who are themselves in trouble. The Christian has before him the example of his Master, of whom we read, 'because he himself has suffered and been tempted, he is able to help those who are tempted' (Heb. ii. 18). Not only do we take courage from the assurance that Christ can help us because He has been through it all before, but we ourselves are spurred on in our own charitable endeavour to stand by our suffering friends and hold out to them hands which themselves have only recently, perhaps, been wounded, and bear their scars still. Paul wrote of this in his letter to Corinth, where he expands this thought in immortal words : 'Blessed be the God and Father of our Lord Jesus Christ, the Father of mercies and God of all comfort, who comforts us in all our affliction, so that we may be able to comfort those who are in any affliction, with the comfort with which we ourselves are comforted by God. For as we share abundantly in Christ's sufferings, so through Christ we share abundantly in comfort too. If we are afflicted, it is for your comfort and salvation; and if we are comforted, it is for your comfort, which you experience when you patiently endure the same sufferings that we suffer. Our hope for you is unshaken; for we know that as you share in our sufferings, you will also share in our comfort' (2 Cor. i. 3–7). One of the great bonds of fellowship of the early Church was their comradeship in suffering (see also 2 Cor. vii. 4–7). For them the sword was drawn up to the gates of heaven, but they stood together and those who had been through the fierceness of opposition were able to strengthen their brethren by their example and encouragement. This is a real ministry of comfort which every Christian must fulfil, but he can hardly do so until he has read the meaning of the word suffering in his own experience. It is certainly greatly honouring to God when the stream of divine comfort flows with increased depth and vigour from hearts that have themselves felt its refreshment, to hearts as yet arid and ignorant of what God can do for them in their distress.

Mary Webb beautifully describes the comfort and cheer that a broken heart can bring to others in trouble in her poem 'A Factory of Peace':

> I watched her in the loud and shadowy lanes
> Of life; and every face that passed her by
> Grew calmly restful, smiling quietly,
> As though she gave, for all their griefs and pains,
> Largesse of comfort, soft as summer rains,
> And balsam tinctured with tranquility,
> Yet in her own eyes dwelt an agony.
> 'Oh, halcyon soul!' I cried, 'what sorrow reigns
> In that calm heart which knows such ways to heal?'
> She said—'Where balms are made for human uses,
> Great furnace fires, and wheel on grinding wheel
> Must crush and purify the crude herb juices,
> And in some hearts the conflict cease;
> They are the sick world's factories of peace.' [1]

The chief sense in which pain can be said to be *ad majorem dei gloriam* lies in the end result of its effect on the personality and character of the sufferer. Paul tells the Ephesians, 'We are his workmanship', part of the handiwork of the Creator God whose plans for the universe cover also a pattern for the individual lives of those who people it. 'He destined us in love to be his sons through Jesus Christ, according to the purpose of his will, *to the praise of his glorious grace*' (ii. 10, i. 5, 6). In the prophecy of Isaiah, there is a similar vision of Israel as the product of God's shaping hand, those who are 'called by my name, whom I created for my glory . . . the people whom I formed for myself that they might declare my praise' (xliii. 7, 21). 'Behold, like the clay in the potter's hand, so are you in my hand, O house of Israel', declares Jeremiah, using the same analogy (xviii. 6). All the divine skill and care that are expended upon the lives of God's children combine to produce, when the subject allows himself to be as pliable as clay in the hand of the craftsman ('Does the clay say to him who fashions it, "What are you making"?', Is. xlv. 9), a finished work of art which brings highest credit upon the One who so devotedly planned

[1] Quoted by J. S. Stewart, *The Strong Name*, p. 166.

and perfected His work. This is the thought uppermost in Robert Browning's mind when he wrote—

> He fixed thee mid this dance
> Of plastic circumstance,
> This Present, thou, forsooth, wouldst fain arrest:
> Machinery just meant
> To give thy soul its bent,
> Try thee and turn thee forth, sufficiently impressed.

The author remembers watching a South Indian potter working at his wheel, fascinated by the skill with which the almost loving interest of the designer in the clay transported it into a thing of beauty and usefulness, a tribute to his genius. The most interesting moment of all in that process was when the potter suddenly stopped the wheel, and we saw him most carefully pick out of the slowly shaping form a speck of grit almost invisible to the naked eye, but likely to be fatal to the symmetry and security of the vessel. Are there not times in the life of God's children when the providential hand of God brings everything to a standstill with a shattering suddenness—a bereavement, a disaster, an illness it may be—and then through this crisis proceeds to take from the life concerned such things as would mar the perfect work upon which God's heart is set? Maybe there are times when we would 'fain arrest' the whirl of life ourselves if we could, for we do not realize the hidden meaning of the rush of circumstances around us. But when God arrests it Himself, it is in order to make a greater beauty of those in whom He is so concerned.

One of the glories of trouble, as seen in this way to be the hand of God at work on the soul, is described by Paul in his letter to Rome : 'We rejoice in our hope of sharing the glory of God. More than that, we rejoice in our sufferings, knowing that suffering produces endurance, and endurance produces character, and character produces hope, and hope does not disappoint us' (v. 2–5). Looking back on a life devoted to God's service, full of experiences which had tested his faith and challenged his devotion to the full, Paul suggests that if we are ever to display the virtue of patience it must be against the dark background of suffering, that character without fortitude is incomplete, and that a crowning hope is the reward awaiting those who at the cost of pain allow God to do His work upon them. And this he says in the context of the cross whither Jesus' endurance took Him, the standard of what is expected of all those who have been justified by His death.

This brings us to consider the suffering that comes to Christians not merely in the general run of experience but particularly on account of their faith. 'He who fears to suffer, cannot belong to Him who suffered,' wrote Tertullian as he urged his fellow believers not to flee their forthcoming persecutions. Our Lord made it clear to His disciples that in following Him they were running into trouble. Those who were to become members of the Head that was to be crowned with thorns, would themselves inevitably feel some pain. With the shadow of the cross creeping relentlessly across His path, Jesus warned His disciples as they sat with Him to share in the last supper; 'Remember the word that I said to you, "A servant is not greater than his master." If they persecuted me, they will persecute you' (Jn. xv. 20). He was but reminding them of what He had declared at the outset of His ministry in the Sermon on the Mount : 'Blessed are you when men revile you and persecute you and utter all kinds of evil against you falsely on my account. Rejoice and be glad, for your reward is great in heaven, for so men persecuted the prophets who were before you' (Mt. v. 11, 12). With this warning went the promise of eternal reward, but it was devotion to the Person of Christ which kept the early Church faithful through persecution, rather than the promise of heavenly gain.

We cannot but be struck by the tone in which the New Testament writers seem to have welcomed their sufferings with open arms. To them it was accepted along with the gift of eternal life, as part of the price to be paid for the privilege of belonging to Christ. 'It has been granted to you that for the sake of Christ you should not only believe in him but also suffer for his sake,' wrote Paul to the Philippians, going on later to say of his own glad sacrifice of himself for Christ, 'Even if I am to be poured as a libation upon the sacrificial offering of your faith, I am glad and rejoice with you all' (i. 29, ii. 17). When Peter and his companions were arrested, put in jail and beaten, we read of them, 'rejoicing that they were counted worthy to suffer dishonour for the name' (Acts v. 41). Paul and Silas sang God's *praises*, of all things, in *prison* of all places, at *midnight* of all times! (Acts xvi. 25). The same spirit shows itself in Peter's letter when he calls on his readers to 'Rejoice in so far as you share Christ's sufferings' (1 Pet. iv. 13). James says 'Count it all joy' because the fruit of character and faith can only be formed through trials (Jas. i. 2–4). Paul declares : 'With all our affliction, I am overjoyed' (2 Cor. vii. 4). The writer to the Hebrews delighted to recount the tale of those whose faith enabled them to endure (xi. 33–40). And the whole emphasis of John's book of Revelation, written as it was from the other side of persecution, after the fall of Jerusalem, is one of glory and triumph. It is important for twentieth-century Christians to realize that the conditions of their witness are still the same as when Jesus said : 'In the world ye shall have tribulation' (AV). Paul, staggering on with intrepid courage after being left by the roadside for dead after being stoned, warned the Church at the next stopping-place that 'through many tribulations we must enter the kingdom of God' (Acts xiv. 22). He never forgot that the Lord had said to Ananias 'I will show him how much he must suffer for the sake of my name' (ix. 16). He urged the Christians at Thessalonica, who had witnessed the rough handling the missionaries had received there, 'that no one be moved by these afflictions. You yourselves know that this is to be our lot. For when we were with you, we told you beforehand that we were to suffer affliction' (1 Thes. iii. 3, 4). Most of us to-day do not have to anticipate the violent opposition which was the lot of the apostles, but we must not allow the easier conditions of modern witness to soften the ardour of our faith, a faith which was handed on to subsequent generations by men marked out to be martyrs.

It is immensely strengthening to one's Christian devotion to read the story of those who down Christian history have emblazoned its pages with tales of heroism and endurance. It is challenging to remember how few of the early apostles died an easy and natural death. In *The Bible Handbook*, Dr. Joseph Angus has thus summarized the New Testament and early Christian tradition of martyrdom : 'Matthew suffered martyrdom by the sword in Ethiopia. Mark died at Alexandria after being dragged through the streets of that city. Luke was hanged on an olive-tree in Greece. John was put into a cauldron of boiling oil but escaped death, and was banished to Patmos. Peter was crucified at Rome with his head downwards. James was beheaded at Jerusalem. James the Less was thrown from a pinnacle of the temple, and beaten to death below. Philip was hanged against a pillar in Phrygia. Bartholomew was flayed alive. Andrew was bound to a cross, whence he preached to his persecutors till he died. Thomas was run through the body at Coromandel in India. Jude was shot to death with arrows. Matthias was first stoned and then beheaded. Barnabas was stoned to death by Jews at Salonica. Paul "in deaths oft", was beheaded at Rome by Nero.'[1]

We hear Tertullian addressing the martyrs of the fourth century : 'Let us drop the name of prison, let us call it a place of retirement. Though the body is shut in, though the flesh is confined, all things are open to the spirit. In spirit, then, roam abroad; in spirit walk about, not setting before you shady paths or long colonnades, but the way which leads to God. As often as in spirit your footsteps are there, so often you will not be in bonds. The leg does not feel the chain when the mind is in the heavens.'[2]

We think of Samuel Rutherford in his Aberdeen jail writing 'Christ and his cross together are sweet company, and a blessed couple. My prison is my palace, my losses are rich losses, my pain easy pain, my heavy days are holy and happy days.'

We skip two centuries and read again the words of that moving letter which reached the headquarters of the Church Missionary Society in 1887 from three survivors of the native king's persecution of the Baganda Christians : 'We are hunted and burned in the fire and beheaded and called sorcerers for the name of Jesus Our Lord. Do thank God who has granted to us to suffer here at this time for the Gospel of Christ.' The same triumphant confidence comes echoing from Uganda's neighbour, Kenya, only two generations later, when, at the time of

[1] Quoted by H. W. Frost in *Miraculous Healing*.
[2] *Ad Martyras*, 1.2.

the Mau Mau rebellion, the Kikuyu Christians sent this message to Britain : 'Tell them that the gates of hell have risen up against Christ's Church among us, and have not prevailed. Tell them that we have experienced the fulfilling of the Lord's promise : "Behold, I have given you authority over all the power of the enemy." Tell them that we love the Lord, and look to Him for all we need. In all things we see His hand.'

We stand amazed at the cool Christian decision of Dietrich Bonhoeffer of Germany when, in 1939, war seemed inevitable, and his many friends urged him to remain in the safety of America. His reply, written to Reinhold Niebuhr, is a classic example of suffering calmly faced for the sake of conscience. 'I shall have no right to participate in the reconstruction of Christian life in Germany after the war if I do not share the trials of this time with my people . . . Christians in Germany will face the terrible alternative of either willing the defeat of their nation in order that Christian civilization may survive, or willing the victory of their nation and thereby destroying our civilization. I know which of these alternatives I must choose; but I cannot make this choice in security.' [1]

No doubt similar instances of brave endurance might be found in the annals of some pagan religious persecutions also. What distinguishes true Christian suffering is the spirit of forbearance and forgiveness with which it is undergone. Jesus' crying 'Father, forgive them; for they know not what they do', was a unique cry. There is nothing comparable to it in the pre-Christian era. Stephen echoed it as the first Christian martyr. In varying degrees of faithfulness since, Christ's disciples have tried to fulfil His word (Mt. v. 44), to return good for evil by blessing and praying for their persecutors. The author will never forget the sensation of kneeling on the floor of a simple African house with three Christian Kikuyu in Kenya, each of them a man marked out by the Mau Mau, and one of them bearing the marks of their recent violence, and listening to them. We prayed together there in the darkness and isolation of their house, and the burden of these wonderful Christian men's prayers was all the same : 'Father, forgive those men

[1] *The Cost of Discipleship.*

hiding away in the forest and threatening our lives. They know no better. They have not seen the light that we have seen. Keep us from being bitter towards them. Have mercy on them, O Lord.'

It is one of Christianity's chief contributions to an age of hatred and variance, that where false accusation is made and undeserved persecution follows, it is taken meekly and borne without resentment. This often means that wickedness triumphs in the immediate situation, but the man or woman of faith knows that neither disfigurement of body nor shortening of life can compare to the corruption of the soul when it is not true to what it believes. There have, of course, been instances in Christian history when the weakness of the flesh has led to the collapse of physical courage in persecution. Jesus understood this in the case of His own closest friends, when they failed to share with Him the torture of Gethsemane and all that followed. He was ready to forgive them, but He expected them not to fail again. Archbishop Cranmer's weakening under the strain of seventeenth-century brainwashing, which caused his enemies to gloat over him, was only temporary. The courage with which he thrust the offending hand into the flames was his true spirit, restored by the grace of God in the hour of need.

Perhaps the extreme test comes when there is a conflict of loyalties, when the persecution of a good man involves suffering, not only for himself, but also for his innocent family or friends. It is hard then to know where a man's duty lies, and quite wrong to condemn from the academic ease of our study the actions of others. Think, for instance, of John Bunyan, whose imprisonment was going to bring such increased suffering on his blind little motherless daughter. Can we not feel the torture of his heart as he cried out, 'Poor child, what sorrow art thou like to have for thy portion in this world! Thou must be beaten, must beg, must suffer hunger, cold, nakedness and a thousand calamities, though I cannot now endure the wind should blow upon thee!' He could have secured release from prison and security for his daughter with a word. But he refused to compromise, and his little child shared something of her father's pain, caught up, whether she understood it or not, in part of the great tragedy of undeserved tribulation because of the wickedness of some men and the goodness of others.

Again, in Millais' famous picture, 'St. Bartholomew's Eve', it will be remembered how the young Huguenot is portrayed standing with his betrothed. This is the testing time of their faith, the eve of their deepest suffering. She has tied round his arm the white cloth, the badge of the Roman Catholics, as his defence against the slaughter threatened for the morrow. But even while he clasps her to himself in deepest affection, he is unfastening with firm fingers the knot her love had tied, determined that if priority must be shown, it must go the way of the spirit rather than that of the heart.

We live in an age when shining examples of this kind of thing stand out in condemnation of our spirit of security at any price. 'Safety first' may be a necessary precaution for the preservation of human life in a mechanical world, but it is fatal when it creeps into the realm of religion. Paul urged on the young Timothy the need to 'take your share of suffering as a good soldier of Christ Jesus' (2 Tim. ii. 3). He reminds him of how he himself is suffering tribulation because of his faithfulness to his commission to publish the word of God (ii. 8, 9). He goes on to encourage him with the assurance that 'If we endure, we shall also reign' (ii. 12). Then from this hint at the royalty of suffering, the honour, dignity and triumph associated with being on the Victor's side, he points out that it is an inevitable portion of the good man's lot, to become a magnet for the attack of the opposition. 'Indeed all who desire to live a godly life in Christ Jesus will be persecuted' (iii. 12). The only way to dodge the cross of Christian discipleship is to dodge the cross of Jesus first. Uninvited pain can never, as we have seen, rightly be regarded as a cross. But when one gladly follows Jesus Christ, knowing the cost in opposition and tribulation, then one begins to understand what He meant when He said, 'Whoever does not bear his own cross and come after me, cannot be my disciple.'

Christian discipleship, then, is a call to arms. The cross, marked on the forehead of the child or adult in the baptism ceremonies of many churches, is a symbol of what it means to belong to Christ. The words that accompany that symbol in the Anglican service can be taken by any devout Christian and made a prayer for himself and all his family, 'in token that hereafter he shall not be ashamed to confess the faith of Christ crucified, and manfully to fight under his banner, against sin, the world, and the devil; and to continue Christ's faithful soldier and servant unto his life's end'.

CHAPTER X

SUFFERING IN THE LIGHT OF THE CROSS

WE have seen earlier that there is a hard-to-define, but none the less real, link between the sins and the sufferings of the world. The Bible makes it clear that the problem of man's sin, and therefore of his sufferings too, was dealt with on the cross. This is the central theme of the Christian faith and it occupies a third of the Gospel stories, and a large part of the Epistles, and is commemorated by every branch of the Christian Church in the broken bread and outpoured wine of the Holy Communion. There is, however, much more to be learned from meditation on the cross than the answer to Job's question, 'How can a man be just before God?' (ix. 2), which is not our present subject.

The cross is the symbol of undeserved suffering. Not only were our Lord's physical pains both acute and lingering; He was suffering even more, innocent as He was, from the shame of His position, Son of God bearing the sins of men. In Gethsemane His sensitive soul seems to have shrunk from what this was going to mean, far more than His body did from the prospect of pain. It is impossible for us to imagine, much less to try in any way to measure, the degree of our Lord's sufferings. We recoil at the apparent injustice of the One who did no sin being made sin for us (2 Cor. v. 21), yet we know He did it voluntarily. We marvel at the way in which He went to the cross and there, by praying for His persecutors, minimized their guilt in the eyes of the world, but made His own humiliation no less hurtful. No-one can understand fully what all this must have meant to Him. We only know there was no other way whereby our sins could be atoned for. In looking at the cross we hope to see some light in the darkness of this mysterious problem of pain, for the Suffering Servant of the prophecies (Is. liii) we believe to have been none other than God Himself. He would not shroud His mightiest act in such mystery that we could understand nothing. He shows us a measure of light, enough for us to live by, and retain our faith. That is what Amy Carmichael had in mind, when she wrote :

> Oh, there are things done in the world today
> Would root up faith, but for Gethsemane.
>
> For Calvary interprets human life;
> No path of pain but there we meet our Lord;
> And all the strain, the terror and the strife
> Die down like waves before his peaceful word,
> And nowhere but beside the awful Cross,
> And where the olives grow along the hill,
> Can we accept the unexplained, the loss,
> The crushing agony, and hold us still.

The first thing that the cross makes clear above all else is that God is love. Whatever appearances may suggest, whatever arguments may be worked out to prove it wrong, however many atheists may raise their voices in disclaiming the existence of a good and loving God, one look at the cross reassures us of this truth. Admittedly, as P. T. Forsyth, writing in the midst of war in 1916, said, 'It is a bold thing in the face of the proud, progressive, aggressive, warlike, Satanic world. It is an act of super-natural courage, in the face of all that today, to believe in the love and grace of God.' [1] But Paul has declared that 'God shows his love for us in that while we were yet sinners Christ died for us' (Rom. v. 8). John has said the same thing. 'God is love. In this the love of God was made manifest among us, that God sent his only Son into the world, so that we might live through him. In this is love, not that we loved God but that he loved us and sent his Son to be the expiation for our sins' (1 Jn. iv. 8-10). We accept their words for they lived close to the truths of which they wrote, and we ourselves have found an echo to it all in the depths of our own hearts.

[1] *The Justification of God*, p. 232.

The cross spells out the love of God in a historic event. It is an emblem raised against every dark horizon to resist the agnostic's denial. Take the cross away, and the darkness of suffering is suggestive of an indifferent God, who having created a world liable to run into trouble, seems to do nothing to help. But when Jesus was lifted up to die, what appeared to the sympathetic bystander an act of sheer cruelty and wicked injustice became the sign by which all men could read that God's love is undeniable. 'God so loved the world, that he gave his only begotten Son' (AV). It is this assurance that enabled Kierkegaard, who, as we have seen, himself suffered intensely for most of his life, to write of it with a measure of real exaltation . . . 'The joy is in this, that now, and every moment, and in every moment to come for ever, there has happened nothing, and there can happen nothing—should even the most shocking horror conceived by the most morbid imagination come true—nothing that can shake the faith that God is love . . . From that it does not follow that faith understands how the working out of the will of God for a man is love. And this is just faith's conflict : to believe without being able to understand.' [1] It is the office of faith to cling to this truth at all costs, brushing aside any doubts that arise, in the spirit of that devout old Quaker, John Greenleaf Whittier, who wrote after a lifetime of struggle against the iniquities of slavery and racial discrimination :

> I see the wrong that round me lies,
> I feel the guilt within;
> I hear, with groan and travail-cries,
> The world confess its sin.

> Yet, in the maddening maze of things,
> And tossed by storm and flood,
> To one fixed trust my spirit clings :
> I know that God is good!

Hezdrel, in *Green Pastures*, when God visits him disguised as a preacher and asks him how he found out that God is a God of mercy, replied, 'De only way anyone kin find it—through sufferin'.' As Hosea traced the

---

[1] *Gospel of Sufferings*, pp. 70, 75.

meaning of suffering love when, at the Lord's command, he took to wife a woman of the streets, presenting to her the active mercy of God, so, by the pains the negro race passed through in America, we get the triumphant note of their 'spirituals', and the closing chorus of this play :

> Hallelujah, King Jesus,
> God of mercy, Lord of love.

The Christian, when faced by the inexplicable, holds to this assurance : that however things may appear, it is for some loving reasons which may be partly hidden from us, that God allows us to suffer. He remembers the Scripture, 'As the heavens are higher than the earth, so are my ways higher than your ways and my thoughts than your thoughts' (Is. lv. 9). He believes unshakably that love is around God's people always, in all circumstances. Whether he feels it or not, he has the assured word of Paul written under the inspiration of God's Spirit, and borne out in the daily experiences of his very disturbed career, that nothing in heaven or earth can separate us from the love of God (Rom. viii. 35–39). Because God demonstrated on the cross the intensity and extensiveness of His love to mankind, no sufferer has any right to say, nor any excuse for saying, 'God can't love me or He would not let me suffer like this.' Whatever explanation there may be for the existence of suffering, one thing will always, in the light of the cross, remain a blasphemy : and that is to deny the love of God, for if God cared enough to suffer on our behalf and win us thereby from our sins to His side, then He must love us indeed.

We have already seen to what extent it is possible to speak of suffering as being the will of God. The cross reassures us that whatever is God's will must be best for us. The pain of the cross, with its tremendous vicarious power ('with his stripes we are healed'), was, in spite of the concentration of sin and suffering that met there, the best thing that could possibly have happened for the world. Shameful and painful death was the will of God for Jesus which He finally accepted in the darkness of that Thursday night in the garden. It was the means of man's salvation. The belief that God is working out His purposes for the very best makes all the difference to us as we bear our own calamities. The process, of course, we cannot be expected to be able to grasp, any more than we can fully understand that cross, limited as we are by finite minds and sinful inclinations. But the fact is there to cling to, as Wordsworth put it :

> One adequate support
> For the calamities of mortal life
> Exists, one only, an assured belief
> That the procession of our fate, howe'er
> Sad or disturbed, is ordered by a Being
> Of infinite benevolence and power,
> Whose everlasting purposes embrace
> All accidents, converting them to good.

In that faith the Christian accepts what comes his way. He is confident that the love of God wills the best for him, and it is the cross which has given him this assurance. The Psalmist sang in the day of his deliverance, looking back on the troubles he had had to endure, 'This God—his way is perfect . . .' (Ps. xviii. 30). The Christian believes this too.

The cross also has something important to teach us about the function of prayer in the setting of trouble. Do we have the right to pray for deliverance? Should our faith lay hold on God until He sets us free? Do our prayers have the power to change God's will? These are urgent and pressing problems to all of us who have held up anxious hands to God in our distresses. Though that great theologian, P. T. Forsyth, as we have seen, argues forcibly that it is an anaemic idea of prayer which denies its power to alter God's will,[1] most of us find this a difficult thing to believe. What we do understand is how prayer can prepare the heart for impending sorrow, as it did when Jesus and His disciples left the upper room to enter the olive groves of Gethsemane. In the quiet there, Jesus had time to seek His Father's face and prepare for the worst. His disciples, too, could have used that time likewise. But when we come to study Jesus on His knees three times seeming to try to change God's will, the lesson for us appears to be that we must be willing to submit to what God allows, rather than try to change it to some-

---

[1] *The Soul of Prayer*, Chapter VII.

thing less exacting. 'My Father, if it be possible, let this cup pass from me; nevertheless, not as I will, but as thou wilt . . . . My Father, if this cannot pass unless I drink it, thy will be done' (Mt. xxvi. 39, 42). One thing that most certainly does arise from contemplating our Lord's agony in the garden is that it was there alone with God that His prayers brought Him the strength to face what was coming, without in any way flinching. His was a courage born of complete surrender to the revealed will of God. Prayer that asks to be spared is prayer to be despised. But prayer that beseeches God to give one the strength not to give up, not to yield, to show no signs of fear, to remain faithful at any cost : that is prayer after the pattern of the Son of God. We must not exaggerate the weight of our burdens, nor bend lower than we need under them. Rather, as Studdert Kennedy put it into the lips of one of his front-line soldiers, meditating on the mystery of the cross, let us seek strength to carry on through everything that comes :

> For 'E felt 'E were doing God's will, ye see,
> What 'E came on earth to do,
> And the answer that came to the prayers 'E prayed
> Were 'Is power to see it through.[1]

A third most vital lesson that we learn from the cross is that death is not the ultimate horror. Much human suffering is due to fear of death, and much is intensified by it. It is noticeable how far more cheerful is the spirit in which the New Testament writers face their sufferings, than that of the Old Testament saints. This may well be that for the former the darkness of the grave had been illuminated, whereas the Psalmists and other pre-Christian writers had for the most part no clear assurance that death did not finish everything. The writer to the Hebrews talks of those whose whole life is haunted by this terror, and who 'through fear of death were subject to lifelong bondage' (ii. 15). Aldous Huxley expresses the same truth in the words of one of his twentieth-century characters : 'If you're a busy film-going, newspaper-reading, football-watching, chocolate-eating modern, then death is hell.'[2] The modern cosmetic industry gambles

---

[1] *Rhymes* 106.   [2] *Eyeless in Gaza.*

its prosperity on woman's insistence on disguising the inexorable advance of years. Death is an evil thing not to be talked about or thought about, but to be pushed into the recesses of the unconscious, there quite possibly to weaken the victim's power even to live.

At the cross, all these views are shown up for what they are, symptoms of an undue reliance on this world and a weak interest in the one to come. 'Death no longer has dominion over him' Paul wrote of Jesus, and the corollary is that we His followers need be under its bondage no longer. Jesus Himself died a young man, hardly having reached the prime of life. Many a modern mourner would weep at the thought of so early a death and erect in the local cemetery that pagan tribute, a broken pillar, symbol of a life 'cut short'. Those of us who believe in a God of love who has a purpose for the life of His children, are immortal until our work is done. We do not have to be old to be able to say, 'It is finished.' Only God Himself, to whom time means nothing, and who measures our lives in terms of character and not longevity, only He knows when His purposes are fulfilled and the moment for our departure is at hand.

The belief that death is 'the porter to the gate of life' is a direct outcome of faith in Christ's atonement on the cross, and the gift of forgiveness of sins which stems from this. For the Christian who has accepted all that this means, 'the sufferings of this present time are not worth comparing with the glory that is to be revealed to us' (Rom. viii. 18–23), when the body itself, the vehicle of suffering and the seat of pain, will be redeemed together with the soul. In the light of this, the evanescent nature of our present pains makes them so much more bearable. 'So we do not lose heart . . . For this slight momentary affliction is preparing for us an eternal weight of glory beyond all comparison' (2 Cor. iv. 16–18). The body may get worn out as years increase, but the spirit draws renewed sustenance day by day. The afflictions which weigh upon us are light when measured against an eternity in which there will be none. In these passages the courageous spirit of the apostle makes light of his many troubles as he dwells upon what comes after death. The Christian understands that a sinful world is bound to 'groan in travail' (Rom. viii. 22), but the redemption which Christ won on the cross is also, he believes, to have a cosmic effect. The whole of God's creation looks forward to the purging of its sin-born pains and stains, and the coming of the new heaven and new earth when God 'will wipe away every tear from their eyes, and death shall be no more, neither shall there be mourning nor crying nor pain any more' (Rev. xxi. 4). With that prospect before him, the New Testament writer could laugh at death in a way we materialists of the twentieth century find inevitably difficult. Yet really it only needs a prayerful pause in the pressure of life to make us face up to the truth Paul so clearly put: to 'be with Christ, . . . is far better' (Phil. i. 23). Is not even the shock of violent death relieved for the Christian by his simple belief that what was true of the penitent thief can be true of him: 'To-day shalt thou be with me in paradise' (AV)?

But this does not mean that the Christian simply sits and sighs for heaven, delectable though that prospect is. The cross itself is the denial of this attitude, for though it is indeed the means whereby the sinner can enter the ultimate and actual presence of God, it has a real message for this life too. The cross condemns sin and all suffering associated with men's evil-doing, and calls on Christians to engage in conflict against every evil thing. The Church, through its leaders and members, must be in the forefront of reform, and direct the community in every effort to lessen the sufferings of mankind. All may not agree as to the best way to set about this, but the sincere disagreements of earnest Christians are a small price to pay for the privilege of taking the cross and its redemptive power to the places where men suffer. The relief of orphans, widows and refugees is splendidly carried on today through Christian bodies. Christian pacifism is a sincere demonstration of the determination to reduce the horrors and sorrows caused by war. Campaigns against racial discrimination demand fullest Christian support in this age when so many of our fellow human beings are only getting part of their share of opportunity, and much mental suffering as well. There are still, in many places, slum conditions crying out for removal. Alcoholism and excessive smoking, death and mutilation on the road : these are the kind of horrors which need a Christian public opinion to reduce their legacy of sadness. No-one deeply concerned about the problem of suffering should be behind in the support of any humane and practical Christian activity which seeks to mitigate such evils.

Jesus bore 'our griefs and carried our sorrows' when He died on the cross, pierced to the heart not only by the cruel thrust of a callous sentry, but more by the sins which cause such an endless tale of misery in the world He loves so much. Out of loyalty to our Saviour we Christians will do most to relieve the trials of others if we learn how to lead our fellow men and women to the cross. There they will see what their sins did to Jesus, and turn away from them in repentance. There they will read of the love of God for men, and catch the infection of it themselves. There they will recognize the place where the great conflict took place with the devil and his powers of darkness, and with other Christians they will gird on their armour to continue the battle against sin and suffering until the day when Satan acknowledges his defeat, and the triumph of the cross is publicly proclaimed at the end of human history.

CHAPTER XI

OUR FINAL ASSURANCE

THERE will undoubtedly be times in the lives of all of us when, in spite of all we know, we are tempted to turn querulously to God and ask : Why? But the true Christian realizes that this is a temptation, for it implies lack of faith in God. We can legitimately say, 'I don't know why', but we have no right, as we have seen, to demand an answer or an explanation. The closer we live to God, the less we feel inclined to question the allowances of His providence. But it does concern Christians when, in times of calamity and troubles, hundreds of their fellow men cry out against the heavens. The fact that this shows how shallow is their faith, and how limited their devotion to the things of God, does not make it any easier for us. Our great longing is to be able to share our faith with those who are not yet committed Christians, and it troubles us to find the problem of pain standing in the way of that discovery. We have tried, therefore, to see what light is thrown by the Bible on the ways of God with men, and we believe that to be forearmed with a measure of clear understanding is of the greatest importance. Those whose 'faith' gives way under the stress of trouble may be those whose confidence was not worth having. One of the main duties of faith is to keep us faithful to our God when we cannot trace any meaning in our afflictions. If we are smitten by suffering before we have any clearly-defined faith it may well be fatal. But on the other hand, if our faith in God is firm in fine weather, it will become, like the wind-swept forest, firmer still in foul.

Our Christian belief is that all things are under the control of divine providence, and that nothing can happen in our lives without some meaning. But we do not expect fully to grasp what this is. Indeed, there will be times when we shall feel like crying out with the patriarch Jacob, 'All these things are against me' (Gn. xlii. 36, AV). He was not to know that a happy ending was just round the corner. He can hardly be blamed for his desperate cry : his beautiful wife Rachel had died giving birth to Benjamin; his old and respected father Isaac had also recently died; his son Judah had turned profligate; there was intense jealousy and unhappiness within his large family; his boy Joseph was apparently dead; Simeon was in jail; the precious Benjamin's life was threatened—all this having come upon a constitution weakened by years of famine and increasing old age. It was not surprising that Jacob felt himself the target of misfortune. But he was judging the situation too soon and without God. He had not yet learnt that 'all things' come under the overruling care of God. While it may not be an explanation, it is the most tremendous comfort to be able to believe that

> All is best, though we oft doubt,
> What th' unsearchable dispose
> Of highest wisdom brings about,
> And ever best found in the close.

Samson grinding at the mill in the company of slaves, his eyes gouged out, and his strength gone from him, must have been near to despair. But thus Milton pictures the chorus of Danites, who have had to watch his afflictions, as still believing in his God, and looking for some good somewhere in his pathetic condition. Actually that life of great promise and then deep disappointment did come to its ultimate fulfilment through suffering.

Paul it is who sums up for us the true attitude of faith. Even though it may appear to Jacob, to Samson, to ourselves that 'all things' are at times 'against us', the Christian veteran reminds his readers, in immortal words: 'We know that *all things* work together for good to them that love God' (Rom. viii. 28, AV). He had, as we have seen, his own thorn in the flesh from which God appeared unwilling to release him; he had been under constant persecution including being stoned within inches of losing his life; he wrote from Philippi to the Corinthians about his 'afflictions, hardships, calamities, beatings, imprisonments, tumults, labours, watching, hunger', though he managed to rise above them by the grace of God, 'as sorrowful, yet always rejoicing' (2 Cor. vi. 4, 5, 10). In the fourth chapter of this same letter he calls his sufferings brief and light (verse 17), but look at the catalogue in full . . . 'far greater labours, far more imprisonments, with countless beatings, and often near death. Five times I have received at the hands of the Jews the forty lashes less one. Three times I have been beaten with rods; once I was stoned. Three times I have been shipwrecked; a night and a day I have been adrift at sea; on frequent journeys, in danger from rivers, danger from robbers, danger from my own people, danger from Gentiles, danger in the city, danger in the wilderness, danger at sea, danger from false brethren; in toil and hardship, through many a sleepless night, in hunger and thirst, often without food, in cold and exposure' (2 Cor. xi. 23-27). It is an amazing record. The ring of assurance in Paul's declaration to the Romans (who were later to need every encouragement in their facing of religious persecution), that everything works together for good, shows the same spirit. It was not only his spirit either. In saying 'we know' he must have had in mind his colleagues in the missionary enterprise who had accompanied him as far as Corinth, and the group of believers in that city whom he gathered round him during his eighteen months there (Acts xviii. 10, 11). All that adventurous band of early Christian pioneers and witnesses knew from experience the truth of those words. They knew, as we also can know, that all things work together for good to those that love God, who have been called and have responded, according to His loving purposes for their lives.

Those who love God, however feebly, can be assured that that love is reciprocated a thousandfold, embracing them, says Paul, in a security which nothing can penetrate . . . 'Who shall separate us from the love of Christ? Shall tribulation, or distress, or persecution, or famine, or nakedness, or peril, or sword? . . . No, in all these things we are more than conquerors through him who loved us. For I am sure that neither death, nor life, nor angels, nor principalities, nor things present, nor things to come, nor powers, nor height, nor depth, nor anything else in all creation, will be able to separate us from the love of God in Christ Jesus our Lord' (Rom. viii. 35, 37–39). The note of triumph in this passage is a challenge to every Christian in trouble to examine himself as to whether he can really say with confidence that *all things*, such as Jacob felt were against him, and Paul says work together for good, are actually our stepping-stones to victory. What keeps a Christian confident and victorious in trouble is not the fact that he has a perfectly clear picture of *how* all things work out for good, but a perfect assurance that none of these things means God does not love him. In the light of this passage, however sharp the pain or however bewildering the apparent problem, Christians must never surrender their belief in the love of God. There is no reason to do so. If we judge the love of God by the imperfect standards of human life, then we may think that suffering and love are inconsistent. We would spare our loved ones all suffering. It does not appear that God does. Must we then argue that He has ceased to love us? Or should we, on the other hand, daringly suggest that He delights in causing pain? Neither of those views are found in the Bible. The sacred record simply reflects the faith of those who were so confident of the love of God that they clung to that through everything. We would do well sometimes to drop our arguments and semi-explanations, and quietly prove our ability to rise through and above our troubles by repeating Paul's magnificent peroration which closes this eighth chapter of Romans, and laying claim to its truth.

It is 'through him who loved us' that Paul tells us we can triumph 'in all these things'. In writing to the Philippian church he uses the same phrase, 'all things', in the context of humiliation, hunger, need and affliction, to say : 'I can do all things in him who strengthens me' (iv. 11–14). This means that in the loving care of God we are never left to face a difficult situation alone or without assistance. It was in the strength of Christ that Paul managed to rise so triumphantly over his troubles, and as Oliver Cromwell once said, quoting this same favourite verse of his, 'He that was Paul's Christ is my Christ too.' We sometimes forget how close our Lord is to us in our sufferings. 'The Lord is at hand' (Phil. iv. 5). When, in his unregenerate days, Paul had been in the forefront of those who made life for the new Christian converts so unbearable, Jesus was so bound up with them in their pains that the question Paul was asked as he knelt on the Damascus road was, 'Why persecutest thou *me*?' Our Lord, as we have seen, suffered more than we ever shall. His compassion, which impelled Him in the days of His life on earth to one kindness after another, is still an essential part of the living, glorified Lord. He is not far from any one of us and when we suffer, He suffers with us too. Speaking of the Church as the Body of Christ, Paul says : 'If one member suffers, all suffer together' (1 Cor. xii. 26). If that is true of each one of us who makes up the Body of Christ, how much more true it is that if the limbs are hurt, the Head will feel it even more. So when we drop on our knees in prayer to seek that divine help without which we can go no further, the first thing we should remember is that Christ feels it too, 'for because he himself has suffered and been tempted, he is able to help those who are tempted . . . For we have not a high priest who is unable to sympathize with our weaknesses, but one who in every respect has been tempted as we are, yet without sinning. Let us then with confidence draw near to the throne of grace, that we may receive mercy and find grace to help in time of need' (Heb. ii. 18, iv. 15, 16).

Whatever form our difficulties may take, we shall find Jesus Christ ready and able to help us. Are we worried by financial loss and anxious for our dependents, tempted perhaps to stoop to unworthy ends in order to find more security? Let us go back to the quiet words spoken on the Galilean hillside in the Sermon which has set the tone of Christian confidence from that day to this : 'Do not be anxious about your life, what you shall eat or what you shall drink, nor about your body, what you shall put on . . . your heavenly Father knows that you need them all. But seek first his kingdom and his righteousness, and all these things shall be yours as well. Therefore do not be anxious about tomorrow, for tomorrow will be anxious for itself. Let the day's own trouble be sufficient for the day' (Mt. vi. 25–34). Perhaps we are burdened with a load of trouble which no-one can take from us, part of it possibly our own fault, much of it undeserved. Are we to carry it alone when the Lord Himself offers to relieve us by sharing it with us, thereby transforming its grievous weight into something easy and light? 'Come to me, all who labour and are heavy-laden, and I will give you rest. Take my yoke upon you, and learn from me; for I am gentle and lowly in heart, and you will find rest for your souls. For my yoke is easy, and my burden is light' (Mt. xi. 28–30). Is it the sinking feeling of impending disaster, the fear of bad news, the awful waiting in uncertainty that seems to sap our power to hold on? Listen to our Lord soothing the distracted disciples in the upper room in just such a situation as that : 'Let not your hearts be troubled; believe in God, believe also in me . . . Peace I leave with you; my peace I give to you; not as the world gives do I give to you. Let not your hearts be troubled, neither let them be afraid. . . . I have said this to you, that in me you may have peace. In the world you have tribulation; but be of good cheer, I have overcome the world' (Jn. xiv. 1, 27, xvi. 33).

We do not suggest that our Lord's chief activity is to bring comfort to the suffering. He is far more engaged in the world seeking to bring forgiveness to the sinning, and defeat to the powers of evil. The Church of Christ, where it is faithful to its Lord, is equally preoccupied. But no-one can deny that again and again the Bible tells us of those who have turned to God as their refuge and strength and found in Him the help and grace and comfort of which they stood so sorely in need. It may be that some-one reading these words just now needs to turn to Christ in this way. Do so as you close this book, and you will find that He will see you through, 'for he has said, "I will never fail you nor forsake you." Hence we can confidently say, "The Lord is my helper, I will not be afraid"' (Heb. xiii. 5, 6).

We began this book, as so many people are tempted to do, by looking at suffering as a problem. We must end it by seeing it as a challenge. Christ did not give an answer while He was on earth to the doubts and queries of those who were faced by the difficulty of reconciling the exist-ence of a loving God with that of calamity, distress and pain. He did not give an answer, and He never received one Himself when His own heart cried out on the cross, 'My God, my God, why?' He did not receive an answer because He was the answer. It is in Christ that we know God loves the world. It was in His derelict cry on Calvary that we can measure something of the depth of that love. Our faith must cling to Him and ask no further questions. We see in the suffering of others a challenge to go out to them in love. We see in our own calamities a challenge to rise through them to greater spiritual heights and a closer walk with God. Faith must not demand an explana-tion even though it may be frail enough sometimes to frame the query, Why?

Robert Louis Stevenson, sitting sick in a darkened room with one arm strapped across him, wrote, 'Whether on the first of January or the thirty-first of December, faith is a good word to end on.' Faith is content to repose upon its knowledge that the things we cannot understand in the imitations of human life have, beyond us and out of time, an explanation in the plans of God. Faith is so sure of the love of God that it accepts the inexplicable and is willing, if need be, never to fathom its meaning. Indeed, the greater the suffering the more demands are put on faith, but it is a faith that is strong because it has its roots, not in vague speculation, but in revealed truth. It knows that God is love and it knows that God's thoughts are higher than our thoughts and His ways than our ways. Faith therefore sees in calamity a challenge to our trust rather than a problem to our intellect, and so the Christian faces the storms of life in the spirit of

One who never turned his back but marched breast forward,
　　Never doubted clouds would break,
Never dreamed, though right were worsted, wrong would triumph,
　　Held we fall to rise, are baffled to fight better, sleep to wake.